amy butler's
piece keeping

amy butler's
piece keeping

20 Stylish Projects that
Celebrate Patchwork

Photographs by
David Butler

CHRONICLE BOOKS
SAN FRANCISCO

Library of Congress Cataloging-in-Publication Data available.

ISBN 978-1-4521-3447-5

Manufactured in China

Text and projects by Amy Butler
Instructions and illustrations by Sheila Brex
Photographs by David Butler
Photo Styling by Monique Keegan's Enjoy Co.
Technical editing by Dolin O'Shea
Designed by Jeri Heiden for SMOG Design, Inc.

Aleene's® Stop-Fraying® fabric sealant is a registered trademark of Duncan Enterprises; Aleene's Jewel-It Washable Glue is a registered trademark of Duncan Enterprises; Biz detergent is a registered trademark of CR Brands, Inc.; Bosal fusible stabilizer is a registered trademark of Scambia Industrial Development; Carol Doak is a registered trademark of C&T Publishing; Clover Wonder Clips is a registered trademark of Clover Mfg. Co., Ltd.; Clubhouse Crafts Natural Cotton Braiding Cord is a registered trademark of Sulyn Industries; Coats threads is a registered trademark of Coats Group PLC; Fairfield Foamology Design Foam with Sticky Base is a registered trademark of Fairfield Processing Corporation; iCraft SuperTape is a registered trademark of Therm O Web, Inc.; Janome Memory Craft 6500 is a registered trademark of Janome Sewing Machine Co., Ltd.; Miyuki Beads is a registered trademark of Miyuki Co., Ltd.; Nature-Fil Blend by Fairfield is a registered trademark of Fairfield Processing Corporation; Nymö shades are a registered trademark of IKEA; Pellon® 806 Stitch-n-Tear is a registered trademark of Freudenberg Nonwovens; Prym-Dritz needles is a registered trademark of the Prym-Dritz Corp; RIT Bright White dye is a registered trademark of Phoenix Brands LLC; 505® Spray & Fix Temporary Fabric Adhesive is a registered trademark of ODIF USA; Wright's twill tape is a registered trademark of Simplicity Creative Group.

10 9 8 7 6 5 4 3 2 1

Chronicle Books LLC
680 Second Street
San Francisco, California 94107
www.chroniclebooks.com

In honor of the creative spirit in all of us!

Contents

Design Influences

Themes, Inspiring Techniques & Handwork

I have a sweet spot for particular patchwork designs, shapes, and techniques, many inspired by traditional motifs like Flying Geese and Log Cabin. In this chapter I get to take you through the influences that make me crazy-in-love with patchwork and handwork, plus I get to dish a little bit about their history and meaning. These themes are the rich inspiration for the projects in this book.

I'm inspired by these classics because they're a wonderful starting point for all kinds of creative play, yet they have their own personalities and charm that can be translated a thousand different ways. I find I'm attracted to repeating symbols, elements, and shapes; they appear often in my creative work: triangles, stripy lines, and energized zigzags! My favorite way to design is improvisational, letting my intuition be my guide and allowing a completely unique art piece to unfold in a spirited way. There's great freedom in creating from this place; it feels like I'm making a painting—one stroke of fabric at a time. I hope you'll find your own special inspirations in this chapter to launch many creative adventures and endless hours of handmade pleasure.

Log Cabin

I really love the wonky and delicious surprises that happen when you design intuitively with the structure of Log Cabin blocks! These traditional blocks exude a playful, rhythmic energy that invites creative interpretation. Historically, Log Cabin quilts come from scrappy beginnings and were often made from recycled or discarded fabrics. The scraps of fabric were sewn to a foundation of muslin or other fabric in place of batting and hand-sewn together through the layers. The Log Cabin pattern is said to have gotten its name from its resemblance to the actual log cabins of the American pioneers just after the Civil War, when it became part of American history. However, the pattern itself has origins that go even farther back. An early nineteenth-century excavation of an Egyptian tomb found the pattern arranged in dyed linen strips around mummies and other objects of royalty. You can gather that the pattern must have been believed to have protective energy to carry the person into the next realm.

The significance of patterns throughout history and how they're carried forward fascinates me! This could be why we have such a strong attraction to the Log Cabin design in blocks and quilts—it's steeped in a mighty, rich history and has had a reason for being for a very long time. The discovery of these patterns in the early nineteenth century sparked a great deal of fascination in Europe and likely could have become the main influence in the Log Cabin working its way into households. It is believed the Amish brought the pattern over from Germany to America, where it then took on a whole new life.

Traditional Log Cabin blocks are made starting with a small piece of fabric as the center block. Strips of fabric are then sewn to this center piece counterclockwise in a sequential order. The strips can vary in shades from light to dark and vary in width. My heart votes for the variations on the traditional theme, leaning toward more freeform interpretations like the Improv Log Cabin, where the strips and squares, though built around a center piece, vary in size and direction as they are sewn. The pattern of the block is designed as it is stitched, with no planning, but comes together by using pure, unadulterated intuition, which I love!

Another variation of the pattern is the Wonky Log Cabin, where the strips and squares going around the center piece are not at right angles but have more of a slant or tilt to them. In both instances, I adore mixing large swaths of interesting fabrics into my Log Cabin quilts, with many of the prints coming from my vintage stash. I find these quilts are the perfect home for these cherished fabrics so I can enjoy them for many years to come. The dynamic and rich juxtaposition of the large fields of graphic prints combined with the rhythm of the Log Cabin design creates a wonderfully odd and totally unique quilt.

You'll see both variations of the Log Cabin reflected in these projects in the book: *Whimsy Quilt* (page 87), *Tapestry Shoulder Bag* (page 98), *Bohemian Wrap* (page 136), *In the Moment Quilt* (page 72), *Improv Pillows* (page 69), *Statement Necklace* (page 95), *Treasure Box* (page 119), *Illumined Lampshades* (page 46), and *Bijoux Belt* (page 146).

Flying Geese

This pattern has some serious age—it dates back several centuries. It is found in Asia and the Middle East in tiles and textiles and also has a strong history in nineteenth-century North American quilts. The quilts were once thought to communicate directions between people who worked for and traveled by the Underground Railroad, which I find fascinating because the triangles represent bird migration and the movement of people.

The Flying Geese pattern is typically made up of a single triangle surrounded by two smaller triangles. The base of the block is twice as wide as it is high, and the larger triangle in the middle represents the goose or bird in flight with its

Heirlooms

a memo from
VELMA HEYMANN

This row is 35 blocks
long. Seems Correct.
11-30-84

Treasures

wings outspread. There is usually a contrast of light and dark between this larger triangle and the two smaller triangles so the "goose" stands out. Sewing many of these blocks together with the larger triangle blocks pointing in the same direction gives the illusion of birds in flight or migration. The blocks can also be arranged so the points of the triangles go in different directions forming squares, stars, pinwheels, or arrows.

This pattern has special meaning for me as it was one of my Grandma G's favorites and I have inherited several of her hand-pieced blocks in progress. I especially treasure a box of her Flying Geese blocks that she hand pieced using scraps of my grandfather's neck ties. The discoveries I made searching through this box are magical for me as many of her handwritten notes were tossed in, including her row design and special construction tips she created to help her complete the quilt. Having inherited this treasure, I set out to make some simple pillows using her beautiful blocks so I can enjoy them forever. Continuing on with my love for "G" and feeling more than a bit passionate about the Flying Geese pattern, I created several fresh projects for *Piece Keeping* that celebrate this wonderful design: *Stash Pouches* (page 112) and *Embellished Infinity Scarf* (page 141).

Triangles

This design form is a kissing cousin to the Flying Geese pattern and that's one of the reasons why I love it! This simple three-sided shape has a long history as an iconic symbol and design motif. Much like the Log Cabin and Flying Geese patterns, the Triangle has a past deeply steeped in symbolism. The Egyptian pyramids are giant triangles that point to the sun, symbolizing the strength, power, and focus of the pharaohs. The three sides of a triangle can represent the body, mind, and spirit. When pointing up, it represents the ascent toward the spiritual world, and when pointing down it represents descent into the physical world. In Morocco, the Triangle motif is found in repeating patterns in architecture, textiles, and pottery, and is understood as a stylized eye or hand meant to protect people from the evil eye.

This is a bit heady, but incredibly interesting! This simple yet mighty shape has found its way into our patchwork world in design arrangements that make up a large part of most traditional quilting patterns. And, when combined with color, the Triangle can make a variety of patterns, ranging from simple and bold to complex and rich. You'll find a bevy of Triangle inspiration while exploring these projects in the book: *Pyramid Pillows* (page 59), *Cozy Patch Floor Cushions* (page 64), *Tribal Cuffs* (page 105), *Talisman Necklace* (page 125), and *Divine Patchwork Dress* (page 131).

Stripes

The stripe might be one of the most commonly used forms in design—and one of the most fun to play with—but don't be fooled by its simplicity. This element can easily be translated into a huge variety of designs that form the basis of such quilting charmers as chevrons, checks, and lattice patterns. When organized, the Stripe becomes the launchpad for a host of patchwork possibilities, but I'm also fond of loose and whimsical applications where the Stripes go off a bit and feel more freeform. These projects in *Piece Keeping* celebrate the energy, elegance, and ease of the Stripe: *Dreamweaver Headboard, Wall Art & Quilt* (page 51), *Wanderlust Quilt* (page 77), *Aspen Branches Quilt* (page 80), and *Tribal Cuffs* (page 105).

Patchwork

Patchwork as a handmade process is at the heart of *Piece Keeping* and a tradition in the textile arts that has made many a life richer through need, utility, love, and creative expression. For those of us who love patchwork, we all have our own way of bringing it into our lives. I grew up with patchwork, admiring my grandmother's quilts, and later found my way back to it through my love of fabric and sewing.

Patchwork's history has early beginnings and can be traced back thousands of years to China, where some of the first samples of cloth being stitched together have been found. Patchwork was probably initially born of necessity where worn fabrics from bed covers and clothing were sewn or "patched" together to make them last longer and make them warmer. For most of history, patchwork quilts and bedspreads were created for pure utility with little concern for aesthetics,

Comfort

but when fabrics became more common, varied, and affordable, patterns started to develop in the patchwork for more decorative purposes. Over the years, as the quilt maker had more leisure time, the patterns and handwork became more intricate, resulting in the creation of family heirloom quilts that get passed down through generations.

Stylistically, patchwork is as varied and unique as the creator. My favorite patchwork to create is spontaneous, with no specific patterns or templates used in making the quilt design, the fabric selection is often random, and the quilt is "built" as it's sewn. This form of patchwork is so appealing to me because of the make-do, creative spirit it holds. Depression Era quilts, Japanese Boro quilts, and the brilliant designs from the women of Gee's Bend all celebrate this process of creating.

Decorative Hand Quilting

Many of the projects in *Piece Keeping* are quilted mostly by machine, but some are created by hand. Quilting is created when patchwork or whole pieces of fabric are layered with additional fabric and sometimes batting and then stitched together. In hand quilting, the stitching is usually a running stitch sewn through all layers with a needle and thread. The technique is hundreds of years old and although it has been practiced in different ways in different parts of the world, it's largely been used as a means of creating warm clothing, bedding, or wall hangings. Over time, some of this stitch work became intricate and highly valued, like, for example, sashiko hand quilting from Japan, which evolved into a very distinct and decorative art form.

Sashiko originated with working class and farm families and is a form of stitching done through two or three layers of cloth using a running stitch. The fabrics used were originally layers of old, worn clothing and other textiles sewn together for warmth and frugality. Reusing fabrics was seen as a spiritual act of humility and prayer, but new fabrics were also not widely available, so it was important to conserve and reuse these textiles. The stitching is worked in different patterns, which were distinct to different regions of the country. You will surely enjoy creating your own distinct stitches using the sashiko style with my *Embellished Infinity Scarf* (page 141) and *Charming Garland* (page 41).

Paper Piecing

If precision is called for, then paper piecing is your process! Paper piecing is a method of quilting that helps make perfect points when sewing small pieces or narrow strips of fabric together. It can be difficult and daunting to sew tight areas successfully if you are using a standard piecing technique or templates. With paper piecing, you machine stitch your fabric onto a paper foundation to form your shapes, then tear the paper away from the back of the fabric when your stitching is complete. If you've not done any paper piecing it might feel like a foreign process, but if you work at it step by step you will be amazed by the quality of work you can produce. There are two methods of paper piecing, one where you trim the seam allowances as you go, and another where you precut the seam allowance before sewing the pieces. Both methods are featured in the book in separate projects. The detail and scale in my *Embellished Infinity Scarf* (page 141), *Tribal Cuffs* (page 105), *Treasure Box* (page 119), and *Stash Pouches* (page 112) would be difficult to achieve without using paper piecing. Let these projects be your entrance into a new technique that will become a handy and well-loved tool!

Appliqué

Appliqué is a technique where a piece of fabric or a decorative patch is sewn to a base fabric and is usually meant to stand out or contrast. The origins of appliqué may have started as a method to cover holes in garments, as the word means "to cover."

Traditional appliqué is done by cutting out simple or intricate shapes and then stitching them to a base fabric. The shapes can be combined or layered to form larger designs. The stitches used to attach the appliqué to the base can be decorative, like a satin stitch or a buttonhole stitch, and are often sewn with a contrasting thread for added dimension.

Appliqué can also be applied with the stitches hidden or invisible so that just the appliqué itself is emphasized. This is how my Grandma "G" worked with appliqué. I remember watching her teach my mom and seeing my mother slip into an intense, focused trance. It doesn't have to be hard, and once you get into your groove you will find that the handwork is very relaxing and meditative. My goal is simpler but no less grand as you will work with the appliqué technique in my *Embellished Infinity Scarf* (page 141) and *Tribal Cuffs* (page 105) projects.

Hand Embroidery

Hand embroidery is a truly ancient art form. It came about perhaps as a method to fix holes and then became a way to elaborately enhance a garment or embellish a piece of cloth. Hand embroidery is usually worked on fabric that is pulled taut inside of a hoop. The design that is being embroidered is lightly drawn onto the fabric and acts as a guide for the stitching. Embroidery thread or floss is then threaded through a large-eyed needle sharp enough to pierce the fabric and big enough to create a hole for the thread to pass through. Hand-embroidery thread is usually untwisted, allowing for the fibers of the thread to give the most sheen or light reflection to the work. Stitches that are commonly used in hand embroidery are the running, satin, and backstitch, although there are hundreds of decorative embroidery stitches to choose from.

We get to play with a bit of hand embroidery in my *Embellished Infinity Scarf* (page 141) and *Tribal Cuffs* (page 105). In both instances, the embroidery work enhances the print designs in the fabrics used and adds beautiful depth, personality, and dimension to the overall project.

Beadwork

I'm drawn to handwork of all kinds, especially embroidery and beadwork. Over the years, I have collected many beaded textiles from all over the world. I find the intricacy and textures in this work very inspiring, and I'm intrigued with the meaning and value that these pieces have with different cultures. Beadwork and hand embroidery have a rather symbiotic relationship in that they both started at about the same time and then evolved together. People have been sewing beads to clothing and textiles for at least five thousand years. Shells, horn, precious stones, bones, wood beads, and pearls have all been used throughout history by different countries and cultures for adornment and religious purposes.

Beadwork is the method of stringing beads to other beads or hand sewing them to fabric, using beading thread or wire and a beading needle. It's used to embellish fabrics and embroidery or to make accessories or jewelry. The beading needle is much finer than a standard needle so that it can pass through the center hole in even the smallest of beads. Long needles allow for several beads to be threaded onto the needle at one time, and shorter needles lend themselves best to more complex and intricate work. A flex-wire needle eye will collapse going through a bead and then reshape itself afterward and works well if the thread is thicker. Special beading and monofilament threads work best, as they are both strong and fine and are designed to withstand the friction that will occur from the beads as they are worn or used.

I can get totally consumed with beadwork. I really enjoy noodling out areas on my sewing projects, so I made sure you get to try your hand at it, too! I have you detail these projects with sections of beading to add a bit of bling and really make your projects shine! Check out the *Bijoux Belt* (page 146), *Talisman Necklace* (page 125), *Tribal Cuffs* (page 105), *Embellished Infinity Scarf* (page 141), and *Statement Necklace* (page 95).

Suffolk Puffs (Yo-Yos)

These are so much fun to make! Once you've made one you'll be addicted. Suffolk puffs are commonly called yo-yos in America, but they originated in Suffolk County, England. The puffs are circles of fabric, which are gathered in on themselves with a basting stitch in order to make a smaller, tighter circle in the middle. What's wonderful about these puffs is that you can make them with small scraps of fabric. You may have seen them traditionally used in yo-yo quilts where the sides of the puffs are stitched one to another and to the surface of a base fabric that can be made into a quilt called Suffolk puff patchwork. These puffs are often used for making accessories and broaches, as they closely resemble flower blossoms.

The version I use on the *Bijoux Belt* (page 146) is super cute because it's stuffed to make the yo-yo more dimensional and decorative.

Beaded and Braided Tassels

Tassels have great texture and add a bit of exotic flavor to decorative projects. Historically, they started as weaving knots used to tie off sections of threads on garments or blankets to keep them from unraveling. They became more decorative over time, especially for the French, who perfected tassel making and turned it into an art form called passementerie.

You can make tassels by matching equal lengths of thread and tying them in the center with a suspended knot, allowing the lengths of thread to hang free. For additional ornamentation, the top part of the tassel can be wound with more threads. In *Piece Keeping*, you get to experiment with making two different kinds of tassels: beaded and braided.

To make beaded tassels, a number of beads are added to each of the hanging threads on your tassel. The top threads are then tied together and pulled through a larger bead. The remaining threads are tied in a knot at the top of the tassel and secured. You will make a beaded tassel in my *Statement Necklace* project on page 95.

To make a braided tassel, you simply braid the loose hanging threads. This makes the threads thicker and stiffer. I added small pom-poms to the ends of the braided tassels in my *Treasure Box* project on page 119 for a more tribal feel.

Getting Started

Fabric, Tools & General Notes

The essentials and everything you need to get your creativity flowing.

Fabrics

As a designer, I'm passionate about materials and, for me, the best part about starting a new project is selecting the fabrics. I enjoy mixing different styles and colors and often work with a combination of vintage and new. Getting to design and sew with my own fabrics is a dream, too! I love mixing a variety of materials because it gives my projects a charismatic edge and makes them completely unique. When selecting fabrics for your projects, choose fabrics you love so your personality, warmth, and spirit can shine through. Make sure the prints you select make your heart sing because you'll be investing a good amount of time in your project, so have fun!

Hunting for vintage fabrics can be quite an adventure, and honestly this is one of the reasons I seek them out. There's a good story behind every piece. I scour antique shops, flea markets, garage sales, thrift stores, and vintage clothing shops. Online there are hundreds of traders and sellers with interesting finds from all over the world. The beauty of using vintage textiles is that you are not only allowing their story to be told in a different way but you are also repurposing and recycling a material source.

New fabrics can be found at fabric and quilting shops. My prints are sold at independent stores globally where you often find the most beautiful collections of designs from a huge variety of incredible artists. See my Resource Guide on page 170 to find great options for shops and sources and to access the "Where to Buy" guide on my website.

Please note, if you are working with a fabric with a directional print, be sure to purchase enough yardage to allow for matching up repeats in the fabric and to keep the designs all going in the same direction on the various parts of your project.

Use and Care of Fabrics, Old and New

All fabrics (new or old) should be washed before you start working with them. Here are a few suggestions to follow to get them prepped.

Vintage Fabrics

Vintage fabrics are charming but sometimes need a little extra special handling to prepare them for use. Some finds will be in excellent condition and it will be easy to gently wash and prep them. Others may have suffered a few years wrinkled up in a bag or starched and folded with intense creases. Due to their abuse, they might have a few fragile areas to avoid. Most cottons and linens can be washed in cold water on the gentle cycle. If your fabric hasn't been exposed to water in a while, soak it in cold water for a day or so to rehydrate the fibers before you clean it. If the fabric seems too fragile to go in the washing machine, yet you just have to use it, hand wash the material in warm water with a mild, phosphate-free soap, gently rinse, and let it air-dry.

Here are some other care tips for vintage fabrics I've picked up along the way:

- You can put discolored cotton and linens through a series of long-term baths in Biz detergent. The process can take several days or weeks, depending on how stained the fabric is. Leave it in the initial bath for a week, agitating regularly. If needed, follow with a second bath for another week. This technique is especially good for yellowed whites.

- Don't put bleach directly on stains; it will turn the fabric yellow and weaken the fibers. Instead, soak soiled or yellowed linens in a sodium per-carbonate solution (like RIT Bright White) or a strong enzyme laundry detergent and HOT water.

- Wash small quilting scraps and other small pieces in a bound cotton bag or pillowcase to keep them from getting torn.

- Not everything needs an arduous cleaning. With some fabrics that have become yellow in storage, you may be able to get away with just a gentle machine washing by cutting away any discolored edges. There's likely good material toward the center.

Vintage Sari Silks

If you're not familiar with Indian saris, they are a beautiful, traditional garment worn by Indian women. The sari is made of a long, rectangular piece of fabric that is worn by wrapping most of it around the body and draping one end over the left shoulder. The part of the fabric that is not wrapped but draped is called the *pallu* (or throw). The *pallu* is usually about a 3-foot (1-m) section that is embroidered or decorated. The other end is of a plain weave and often one or two decorative borders will run the length or part of the length of the material.

I have been purchasing vintage saris and incorporating them into my jewelry, garments, and quilts. They are incredible to work with, the colors and patterns are wildly inspiring, and they are very affordable. You get, on average, 4 to 9 yards (4 to 8 m) of fabric, with each sari having a width around 42 to 45 inches (105 to 115 cm). I have a few projects in the book that use sari silk, so I want to give you some suggestions on how to prep and care for your material before sewing with it. Silk is a protein, so it can shrink; it should be prewashed before you sew.

As with other vintage fabric, be mindful that your sari may have worn or torn areas to work around. Hand wash in cold water with mild detergent and roll up the fabric in a towel to remove the excess water, never wringing or twisting the fibers. Air-dry the silk by laying it flat or hanging it up. When dry, use the medium setting on your iron to press out the silk.

The silky fabric of a sari tends to move around when cutting. Here are some things you can do to minimize this:

- Use serrated scissors or layer the fabric with tissue paper when cutting.

- Instead of sliding a ruler across the fabric, lift and place it as you measure and cut the material.

- Before sewing, apply a little spray stiffener to the silk. Be sure to follow the manufacturer's instructions on the spray and test a small area before applying across the whole surface of the fabric.

- Use fine-point, sharp silk pins.

- Use a 70/10 fine sewing machine needle.

- Use a high-quality 100 percent polyester thread.

New Fabrics

To preshrink your material, make a small diagonal clip from each corner of the fabric about ½ inch (1.3 cm) toward the center before washing and drying to help prevent fraying and tangling. Then dry and press before sewing.

Notions and Trims

The projects in *Piece Keeping* specify the trims and notions needed to embellish them. You can find what you need at your local fabric shop, but it's always good to be on the lookout for special one-of-a-kind trims, beads, and embellishments to build a collection that really speaks to you and is ready to inspire you when the mood strikes you to create something. I often find unique vintage trims and buttons at garage sales, charity shops, and flea markets. Vintage Indian sari silk and French ribbons, English buttons, and vintage jewelry can bring an Old World charm to your modern designs. Scour bead shops, hobby stores, and ethnic shops for unusual finds that make your project unique and stylish.

See the Resource Guide (page 170) for recommended material sources.

Basic Tools Needed

Each project has a specific materials list to get you started with minimum fuss. In addition, there are some basics listed here that I assume you have on hand as you'll need them for most projects. If you've done much sewing, you probably have all or most of these, but it's worth taking a little time before you get the urge to sew to make sure you've gathered your supplies and that everything is in good working order.

Fabric marker or chalk pencil
Ironing board and iron
Pressing cloth
Rotary cutter, ruler, and mat
Rulers
Scissors
Seam ripper
Sewing machine needles (universal size 80/20 can be used for most projects, unless stated otherwise)
Straight pins
Tape measure

General Notes

- Be sure to have the basic tools on hand before starting a project. Additional tools needed are listed at the beginning of each project.

- Terms defined in the Glossary and Techniques section (page 164) are marked with an asterisk (*) the first time they appear in a project.

- Please read through all of the instructions before you get started.

- See the Glossary and Techniques section (page 164) for quilt assembly, binding instructions, and general sewing information and techniques.

- All yardage given is for a one-way design. Allow extra yardage for matching or centering a design on your fabric.

- Backstitch at the beginning and the end of each seam for garment or project construction.

- All seam allowances are noted at the beginning of each project.

- Be sure to preshrink your material before sewing.

- Follow the manufacturer's instructions closely when applying fusible interfacing and fleece. If you experience any puckering of the fabric, gently pull back the interfacing or fleece while it's still warm and reapply. Use a damp pressing cloth and the "wool" setting on your iron during the application.

Nesting

Eclectic Wares
for Modern Interiors

Beautiful colors and textures abound in this fresh and stylish homeware section. Decorative garlands, lovely lampshades, cozy quilts, and punchy pillows all make it easy to update your living space and display your new family heirlooms.

Charming Garland

Finished Garland lengths (excluding the tassels): Long Garland: 17 circles – 56" (142 cm); Short Garland: 13 circles – 40" (101 cm);
Tassel length: 25" (64 cm)

Hang this happy garland in just the right spot so you are greeted by its joyful energy whenever you pass by.
Or place it on a tabletop to add a celebratory flair to your next gathering. Easily made to just the right size for you, too!

NOTES
All seams are ¼" (0.5 cm) unless otherwise stated.

DESIGN INFLUENCE
Triangles

TECHNIQUE USED
Sashiko

MATERIALS LIST
Notes: The yardage listed is for making both the garlands and the
tassels at their full lengths. The Long and Short Garlands are
made from the same prints/circles in the same order except
that the Long Garland has four additional prints/circles added
to the bottom. The garland can be lengthened or shortened
by adding or subtracting circles. Measure the area where you
wish to hang the garland and adjust to suit your space. Follow
the sizes in Table 1 for the order of the circle sizes or choose
your own order and number of circles.

Fabrics
From 44" (112 cm) wide light- to mid-weight fabric
Note: I used small amounts of 25 different fabrics, but you can
use fewer and repeat fabrics to get the look you want.
⅛ yard (0.1 m) each of 1 print and 2 solid fabrics for the 2"
  (5.1 cm) Circles
⅛ yard (0.1 m) each of 1 print and 1 solid fabric for the 3"
  (7.6 cm) Circles
¼ yard (0.25 m) each of 4 prints and 1 solid fabric for the 4"
  (10.2 cm) Circles
¼ yard (0.25 m) each of 2 prints and 3 solid fabrics for the 5"
  (12.7 cm) Circles
¼ yard (0.25 m) each of 2 prints for the 6" (15.2 cm) Circles
⅛ yard (0.1 m) each of 8 solid fabrics for the Tassels and Strands

OTHER SUPPLIES
2 packages of 36" x 20" (91.4 x 50.8 cm) double-sided fusible
  heat-moldable stabilizer (by Bosal)
1 spool of coordinating all-purpose thread (Coats)
1 spool of coordinating carpet and button thread (Coats)
8 skeins of different colored coordinating embroidery floss for
  hand stitching (Coats)

ADDITIONAL TOOLS NEEDED
Masking tape and marker
Heavy-duty scissors for cutting stabilizer
Pinking shears
Hand-sewing needle
2 sheets of printer paper
1" (2.5 cm) thick x 7" (17.8 cm) square piece of Styrofoam
Tailor's awl (Prym-Dritz)
Hand-embroidery needle (size 7/9) (Prym-Dritz)
Denim needle 90/14 for sewing through stabilizer
Hair dryer

1 Cut Out the Pattern Pieces
From the pattern sheet included with this book, cut out:
  2" (5.1 cm) Circle
  3" (7.6 cm) Circle
  4" (10.2 cm) Circle
  5" (12.7 cm) Circle
  6" (15.2 cm) Circle
  Garland Tassel

2 Cut Out the Fabric and Stabilizer Pieces
Garland Circle Fabrics

a. Lay your fabrics out in front of you in your desired order.
Label each numerically with masking tape and a marker to
keep track of the order.

b. Fold each fabric for the Garland Circles **right** sides
together, matching the selvages*.

c. Following Table 1 on page 42, trace the Circle patterns four
times onto each fabric, making sure to leave ½" (1.3 cm)
space between them to add seam allowance. Note: Trace
the pattern only twice for Circles 14 to 17. Circles 1, 3, 5, 6, 9,
13, and 15 are the solid fabrics. The remaining Circles are
print fabrics.

d. Using a ruler and fabric marking pen, add a ¼" (0.6 cm)
seam allowance to all of the Circles.

e. Place a pin at the center of each traced Circle to keep the
cut Circle pairs together. Since the fabric is folded in half
(Step 2b), you will automatically cut two for each Circle
traced.

Garland Circle Stabilizer

Following Table 1, spacing them as closely together as possible, trace four Circles for each size onto the stabilizer; for pieces 14 to 17 (the shaded columns) trace two Circles for each size. Cut out each Circle using your heavy-duty scissors. Stack them in piles until ready to use.

Garland Tassels and Strands

Each Garland has nine Tassels hanging from the bottom and one to attach the Strands to the last Garland Circle.

From the 8 solid fabrics:
Cut 20 Garland Tassels

From the remaining fabric:
Cut 19 Strands: 1" x 24" (2.5 x 60 cm)

3 Make the Garland Circles

a. Mark an opening of 1½" to 2" (4 to 5 cm) along the edge on each Garland Circle pair.

b. Starting and stopping at these marks, stitch along the traced line, leaving an opening.

c. Trim off raw fabric edges, about ⅛" (0.3 cm) from seam with pinking shears.

d. Once the Circles are sewn and trimmed, turn **right** side out.

e. To insert the corresponding stabilizer into the Circle, roll the stabilizer into a small tube and insert it through the opening, then unroll it and move it into place. This is a tight squeeze, so patiently work each piece to fit.

f. To close the opening in the Circle, fold one side of fabric over the interfacing edge. Turn under the remaining side along the seam line, folding it to match the shape of the Circle; finger press* to create a nice edge. Slipstitch* the opening closed.

g. Following manufacturer's directions for the stabilizer, press each of the finished Circles. This will lightly bond the fabric to the stabilizer.

h. Sort the Circles into matching sets of two.

TABLE 1 *Trace and cut 4 except where shaded, cut 2*	
Circle #1	4" (10.2 cm)
Circle #2	4" (10.2 cm)
Circle #3	2" (5.1 cm)
Circle #4	6" (15.2 cm)
Circle #5	5" (12.7 cm)
Circle #6	3" (7.6 cm)
Circle #7	4" (10.2 cm)
Circle #8	5" (12.7 cm)
Circle #9	2" (5.1 cm)
Circle #10	4" (10.2 cm)
Circle #11	4" (10.2 cm)
Circle #12	6" (15.2 cm)
Circle #13	5" (12.7 cm)
Circle #14	2" (5.1 cm)
Circle #15	5" (12.7 cm)
Circle #16	5" (12.7 cm)
Circle #17	3" (7.6 cm)

4 Hand Stitch the Solid Fabric Circles

a. Trace each size Garland Circle pattern onto the printer paper. Use Figure 1 as a guide and draw a spiral onto each traced Circle, keeping the lines about ¼" (0.6 cm) apart. Then, mark dots evenly spaced along this line ¼" (0.6 cm) to ⅜" (1 cm) apart. This will be your template for hand stitching. Cut each Circle out.

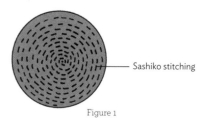

Sashiko stitching

Figure 1

b. Select one solid fabric Circle from each set of two to be hand stitched.

c. Place the first solid fabric Circle onto the piece of Styrofoam. Lay the corresponding sized template on top, matching the edges. Use a few pins to hold.

d. Starting at the center and working out, use a sharp, tapered awl and begin punching each of the dots along the spiral, going through the template and all layers of the circle. Make sure to go deep enough for the hand-embroidery needle to pass through easily. Add more pins as you work if necessary to hold the template and Circle in place.

e. Repeat Steps 4c and d for the remaining solid fabric Circles.

f. Thread your hand-embroidery needle with all of the strands of the first color of embroidery floss that you choose. Make a knot at the bottom of one end.

g. Starting in the center of the first Circle, sew a running stitch* through all of the holes. When you reach the last hole along the outside edge, tie a knot close to the fabric.

h. Repeat with the remaining colors of embroidery floss and circles.

5 Make the Tassels and Strands

a. For each Garland Tassel, align the short straight edges **right** sides together and stitch a ⅛" (0.3 cm) seam down the straight edge. Leave the **wrong** side facing out.

b. Fold each Strand in half lengthwise with **wrong** sides together and press. Open and fold the long edges in to meet the center crease; press again. Pin the folded edges together and edge stitch*.

c. Select one Strand piece for the Hanging Loops at the top of the Garland and cut two 3" (7.6 cm) pieces; set them aside for now.

d. From the remaining Strands cut two of the following lengths:

24" (61 cm)

13" (33 cm)

22" (55.9 cm)

19¼" (48.9 cm)

18" (45.7 cm)

16" (40.7 cm)

9½" (24.1 cm)

14½" (36.8 cm)

20½" (52.1 cm)

e. Insert one Strand into one Tassel through the wide opening up through the smaller opening, having the edges meet. There will be a small amount of excess in the opening. Finger press a pleat to flatten, then stitch across the top edge of the Garland Tassel with a ⅛" (0.3 cm) seam. (See Figure 2.)

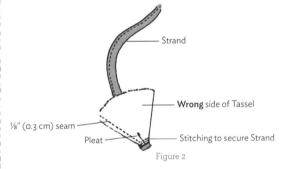

Strand

Wrong side of Tassel

⅛" (0.3 cm) seam

Pleat

Stitching to secure Strand

Figure 2

f. Now flip the Tassel **right** side out. Lightly press the seam on the Tassel.

g. Repeat for the remaining Tassels and Strands for both Garlands, reserving two Tassels for attaching to Garlands.

h. Bring one each of the nine different Strands together for each Garland, matching all of the raw ends. Stitch across the ends with a ½" (1.3 cm) seam to join. To reduce bulk, trim the excess seam allowances on all but two Strands in the center.

i. With one of the remaining Tassels **right** side out, tuck the combined Strand ends up inside, matching the raw Strand edges with the top smaller opening of the Tassel. Machine baste* across the top about ¼" (0.6 cm) from the edge. Repeat with the second remaining Tassel and combined Strands.

Finish the Garland

a. Change the sewing machine needle on your sewing machine to the Denim 90/14.

b. Take one of the Hanging Loops you set aside in Step 5c and fold in half, matching the raw edges. Place these ends about ⅜" (1 cm) in from the edge of one of the top Circles. Stitch securely, going over the stitching several times. (See Figure 3.)

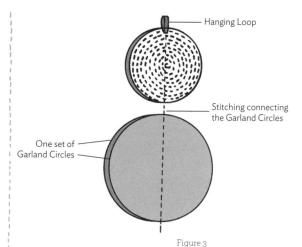

Hanging Loop

Stitching connecting
the Garland Circles

One set of
Garland Circles

Figure 3

g. Repeat with the second set of Garland Circles.

h. To shape the Circle Sets into 3D spheres, set your hair dryer on the highest setting. Working with one set of Circles at a time, heat one side of the Circle for about 10 seconds and then fold the Circle along the stitch line, making sure it forms a 90-degree angle. Hold the Circle in place while it cools. Flip the set over and repeat on the opposite side of the other Circle. Repeat for all of the Circles. (See Figure 5.)

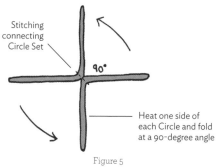

Cross View of Garland Sphere

Stitching
connecting
Circle Set

90°

Heat one side of
each Circle and fold
at a 90-degree angle

Figure 5

c. Repeat with the second top circle of the Garland and Hanging Loop.

d. To attach the Tassels to the Garland, place the top raw edge of the Tassel about ¼" (0.6 cm) in from the bottom edge of one of the last Circles. Stitch securely in place. Repeat with the second bottom Circle and Tassel. (See Figure 4.)

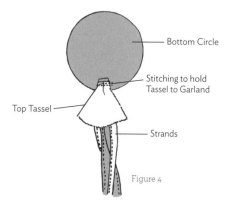

Bottom Circle

Stitching to hold
Tassel to Garland

Top Tassel

Strands

Figure 4

e. On each matching set of Circles (from Step 3h) use your chalk pencil and ruler and draw a line down the center of one Circle.

f. To join the Circles together to make the Garland, first switch your needle and bobbin thread to the carpet and buttonhole thread in your machine. Change the stitch length on your machine to the longest setting. Start with the top set of Circles on the first Garland by placing them together with the marked Circle on top, sandwiching the raw edges of the Hanging Loop in between. Stitch slowly through all the layers following the drawn center line. When you get to the bottom of the first Circle, backstitch* and take a few stitches off the edge and then line up the next set with the drawn line on top. Continue sewing each set in order until you get to the bottom pair. Sandwich the top Tassel and Strands in between the two circles and slowly backstitch when you get to the end.

Illumined Lampshades

Finished sizes: Large – 23" (58.4 cm) diameter x 14" (35.6 cm) tall; Small – 15" (38.1 cm) diameter x 12" (30.5 cm) tall

Modern chic meets patchwork with these customizable shade covers, making it easy to light up your spaces with the warmth of handmade!

NOTES

All seams are ¼" (0.6 cm) unless otherwise stated. The seam allowance is included in all measurements.

DESIGN INFLUENCE

Wonky Log Cabin

TECHNIQUE USED

Patchwork

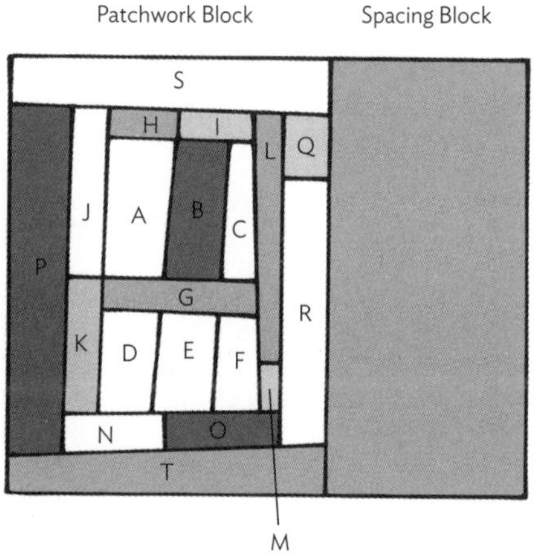

Patchwork Block   Spacing Block

Figure 1

MATERIALS LIST

Note: Fabric and notion requirements are for the shade sizes used; adjust as necessary to fit the lampshade you have. The instructions are written for any size barrel-shaped lampshade.

For the Large or Small size:

Fabrics

From 44" (112 cm) wide light- to mid-weight fabric

⅛ yard (0.11 m) each of 14 different prints for the patchwork blocks

½ yard (0.46 m) of chambray for the spacing blocks

OTHER SUPPLIES

2 packages of ½" (1.3 cm) wide photo-safe double-sided adhesive tape (iCraft SuperTape)

3 packages of ½" (1.3 cm) wide white twill tape (Wrights)

Barrel-shaped plain lampshade (Nymö shades from IKEA have the dimensions given above)

1 package of freezer paper

1 bottle of Aleene's Stop-Fraying, 4 oz. (118.3 ml) or other fabric sealant

1 spool of all-purpose thread in a neutral color (Coats)

10 spring clothespins (Clover Wonder Clips)

ADDITIONAL TOOLS NEEDED

Photocopier

Pencil

24" (61 cm) long rotary cutting ruler

1   Make the Patchwork Block Templates*

a. Measure and record the height and circumference of your lampshade.

b. Add a total of ½" (1.3 cm) to the height measurement for top/bottom overlap. This value will be used as the height of the lampshade in the rest of the instructions.

c. Cut out the Illumined Lampshade Patchwork Block from the pattern sheet included with this book. Use a photocopier to enlarge or reduce the template so the height matches the value above.

d. Measure and record the width of the Patchwork Block.

e. Using a pencil and ruler, trace and label each piece of the pattern onto the dull side of the freezer paper, leaving space between them to add seam allowance.

f. Add a ¼" (0.6 cm) seam allowance to the outside of all pieces. Then cut out each template on the seam allowance line.

2   Cut Out the Fabric Pieces

a. Calculate the number of Patchwork Blocks on the lampshade: Divide the lampshade circumference in half, and then by the width of the Patchwork Block. Round this value up to the next whole number. For example: If the lampshade circumference is 73½" (186.7 cm) and the

Patchwork Block width is 10½" (26.7 cm), the equation looks like this:

73½ (186.7) ÷ 2 = 36¾ (93.4) ÷ 10½ (26.7) = 3½ (3.5)

Rounded up, the next whole number is 4. So, in this example, the lampshade will have four Patchwork Blocks. Whatever number of blocks you calculate for your lampshade, we'll call that number x for the cutting below.

b. Cut the appropriate pieces from your print fabrics as follows:

From Print 1, cut x of each of the following templates:
    Template B
    Template E
    Template G
    Template H

From Print 2, cut x of each of the following templates:
    Template A
    Template C
    Template D
    Template F

From Print 3, cut x of Template I
From Print 4, cut x of Template J
From Print 5, cut x of Template K
From Print 6, cut x of Template L
From Print 7, cut x of Template M
From Print 8, cut x of Template N
From Print 9, cut x of Template O
From Print 10, cut x of Template P
From Print 11, cut x of Template Q
From Print 12, cut x of Template R
From Print 13, cut x of Template S
From Print 14, cut x of Template T

c. Calculate the finished size of the Spacing Blocks: Divide the circumference of the lampshade by x, then subtract the Patchwork Block width. This is the finished width of the Spacing Blocks. For example: If the lampshade circumference is 73½" (186.7 cm) and the Patchwork Block width is 10½" (26.7 cm) and x is 4, then the finished width is found as shown:

73½ (186.7) ÷ 4 = 18⅜ (46.7) – 10½ (26.7) = 7⅞ (20).
(73½ ÷ 4) – 10½ = 7⅞.

d. Add seam allowances and cut Spacing Blocks as follows: Take the width of the Spacing Block from Step 2C and add ½" (1.3 cm). Take the height of the lampshade and add ½" (1.3 cm). This is the cutting measurement for your Spacing Blocks. Cut x of them from the Spacing Block fabric.

 Make the Patchwork Block

a. On a flat surface lay out one of each Template piece as shown in Figure 1.

b. Sew the following pieces together and place back into the layout. Press the seam allowances to one side:

A – B – C
D – E – F
H – I
J – K
L – M
N – O
Q – R

c. Continue sewing the block together in the following order:

ABC – HI
DEF – G
ABCHI – DEFG
JK – ABCDEFGHI – LM
ABCDEFGHIJKLM – NO
P – ABCDEFGHIJKLMNO – QR
S – ABCDEFGHIJKLMNOPQR – T

d. Repeat these steps on each of the remaining blocks needed for your lampshade.

 Complete the Lampshade Fabric Panel

a. Sew one Patchwork Block and one Spacing Block together along the right edge of the Patchwork Block. Press the seam allowance toward the Spacing Block. Repeat with the remaining Patchwork Blocks and Spacing Blocks.

b. Next sew all the block pairs together to form one long panel. Press the seam allowances toward the Spacing Blocks.

c. Fold and press the top and bottom raw edges of the fabric panel under ½" (1.3 cm) to the **wrong** side. Then fold and press the left edge of the fabric panel under ¼" (0.6 cm) to the **wrong** side.

 Attach the Fabric Panel to the Lampshade

a. Apply the double-stick adhesive tape to the inside top and bottom edges of the lampshade, lining up the edge of the shade with the edge of the tape. If your lampshade has spokes attaching it to the center of the lamp, apply the tape to the shade between the spokes.

b. Apply a length of tape on the outside of the lampshade along the right-hand side of the lengthwise seam. Repeat and apply tape along the left-hand side of the seam. (These two tape lines should butt up to each other.) All tape pieces should still have the backing paper attached.

c. Remove the backing paper from the tape on the right-hand side of the lengthwise seam. Place the folded left edge of the Fabric Panel along the left-hand edge of the exposed tape, lifting the folded top and bottom edges over the top and bottom of the lampshade. Finger press* to stick the fabric to the tape.

d. Continue to attach the Fabric Panel around the circumference of the lampshade, connecting the folded top and bottom edges to the inside of the lampshade. The raw edge of the Fabric Panel should overlap the fixed folded edge by at least ¼" (0.6 cm). Temporarily hold the Fabric Panel in place along the top and bottom of the lampshade with the Wonder Clips.

e. Make any adjustments to the fit of the panel on the shade. Pull the top and bottom folds toward the inside of the shade to remove any excess fabric.

f. Once the Fabric Panel is lying correctly, starting from the left edge of the Fabric Panel and stopping 2" (5.1 cm) from the right edge, work in sections to remove the clips and backing paper from the tape and press the fabric into place around the top and bottom of the inside of the shade. If the lampshade has spokes at the edge, as you approach the spoke, gradually fold under the raw edge so that a folded edge lies across the top of the spoke and the seam allowance adjusts back to ½" (1.3 cm) on either side.

g. Fold under and finger press the right raw edge of the Fabric Panel so that it meets the left folded edge. Remove the backing paper from the tape on the left side of the seam and adhere the right folded edge along the right edge of the tape. Finish fastening the fabric into place around the top and bottom edges of the shade.

h. To cover the raw fabric edges inside the lampshade, apply double-stick adhesive tape around the top and bottom inside edges so that it is mostly on the fabric but overlaps the raw edge by approximately ⅛" (0.3 cm). If there are spokes, cut and place the tape between the spokes.

i. Remove the backing paper from the tape and adhere the twill tape to the double-stick tape. Apply Stop-Fraying to the cut edges of the twill tape to prevent raveling.

Dreamweaver Headboard, Wall Art & Quilt

Create these bold, modern blocks for your wall! Whether in the bedroom or elsewhere in your abode, these beautiful handmade works of art complement all of your living spaces. Whenever you're in the mood for a different fabric combination or color, the construction of these wall blocks makes it super easy to swap out for new styles. Stitch a few more blocks together and make a quilt to boot!

NOTES

All seams are ¼" (0.6 cm) unless otherwise stated. The seam allowance is included in all measurements.

DESIGN INFLUENCE

Stripes

TECHNIQUE USED

Patchwork

Headboard and Wall Art

Finished size for Headboard using four squares: 48" x 48" (122 x 122 cm)

Patchwork Square

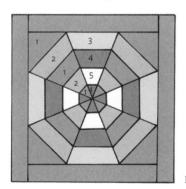

Figure 1

MATERIALS LIST

Note: Yardage and supplies listed are for four Patchwork Squares.

Fabrics

From 44" (112 cm) wide light- to mid-weight fabric
2⅜ yards (2.5 m) of Fabric 1 for Patchwork
2 yards (1.7 m) of Fabric 1 for Side Panels
1¼ yards (1.1 m) of Fabric 2 for Patchwork
¾ yard (0.69 m) of Fabric 3 for Patchwork
1¼ yards (1.1 m) of Fabric 4 for Patchwork
¾ yard (0.69 m) of Fabric 5 for Patchwork

OTHER SUPPLIES

1 spool of coordinating all-purpose thread (Coats)
4 pieces of Foamology Design Foam with Sticky Base 24" (61 cm) square (Fairfield)

 Cut Out the Pattern Pieces

From the pattern sheet included with this book, cut out:
Patchwork Triangle A
Patchwork Triangle B

Cut Out the Fabric Pieces

Use your rotary cutter, mat, and ruler to cut the specific amounts listed below.

For the Patchwork
From Fabric 1

Cut 6 strips – 6" (15.2 cm) x width of fabric* (wof)
Cut 6 strips – 3½" (8.9 cm) x wof
Cut 6 strips – 4" (10.2 cm) x wof

From Fabric 2

Cut 12 strips – 3½" (8.9 cm) x wof

From Fabric 3

Cut 6 strips – 3½" (8.9 cm) x wof

From Fabric 4

Cut 6 strips – 3½" (8.9 cm) x wof
Cut 6 strips – 4" (10.2 cm) x wof

From Fabric 5

Cut 6 strips – 3½" (8.9 cm) x wof

For the Side Panels
From Fabric 1

Cut 16 strips – 4" (10.2 cm) x wof

Then, recut these 16 strips as follows:

Cut 8 strips – 4" (10.2 cm) x 24" (61 cm)
Cut 8 strips – 4" (10.2 cm) x 31½" (80 cm)

Sew the Patchwork Strips

Note: A Strip Set is a set of Strips stitched together in the order indicated to make a pieced fabric length.

For Strip Set A

a. On a large, flat surface lay out three strips of Fabric 1 and two strips of Fabric 2 **right** sides facing up from top to bottom in the following order. (See Figure 2.)

Note: The measurements along the right side of the illustration are the strip measurements before they are sewn together.

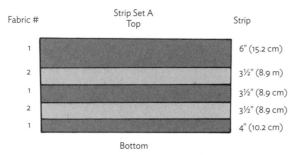

Fabric #	Strip Set A Top	Strip
1		6" (15.2 cm)
2		3½" (8.9 m)
1		3½" (8.9 cm)
2		3½" (8.9 cm)
1		4" (10.2 cm)
	Bottom	

Figure 2

b. Tip: When stitching the Strips together, start sewing at alternate ends to avoid the Strips getting distorted and curving like a rainbow. Start by pinning the first two strips (6" [15.2 cm] of Fabric 1 and 3½" [8.9 cm] of Fabric 2) **right** sides together, matching the long edges, and stitch. Press the seams in one direction.

c. Pin the third strip (3½" [8.9 cm] of Fabric 1) to the second and stitch along the pinned edges. Press the seams in one direction.

d. Continue this process of sewing and pressing the Strips to complete the set.

e. Repeat Steps 3a to d five more times to make 6 Strip Set A's.

For Strip Set B

a. On a large, flat surface, lay out strips of Fabrics 3, 4, and 5 **right** sides facing up from top to bottom in the following the order. (See Figure 3.)

Note: The measurements along the right side of the illustration are the strip measurements before they are sewn together.

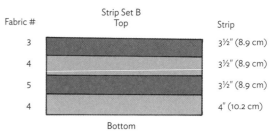

Fabric #	Strip Set B Top	Strip
3		3½" (8.9 cm)
4		3½" (8.9 cm)
5		3½" (8.9 cm)
4		4" (10.2 cm)
	Bottom	

Figure 3

b. Repeat Steps 3b to e for Strip Set A to sew these fabrics into 6 Strip Set B's, pressing the seam allowances in the opposite direction than Strip Set A.

 Use the Pattern Pieces to Cut Out the Triangles

a. Trace and then cut out 16 Patchwork Triangle A's from the Strip Set A's, matching up the placement lines with the seams on the Strip Sets. You can cut up to 3 Triangle A's from each Strip Set.

b. Trace and then cut out 16 Patchwork Triangle B's from the Strip Set B's, matching up the placement lines with the seams on the Strip Sets. You can cut up to 3 Triangle B's from each Strip Set. (See Figure 4.)

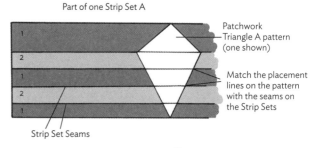

Part of one Strip Set A

Patchwork Triangle A pattern (one shown)

Match the placement lines on the pattern with the seams on the Strip Sets

Strip Set Seams

Figure 4

Sew the Triangles Together to Make the Patchwork Squares

Tip: Finger press* all the seams between the Triangles to keep them from stretching.

a. Pin one Triangle A long edge to one Triangle B long edge, **right** sides together, matching the seams and offsetting the seam allowances. Stitch together, sewing from the point to the wide end of the Triangles. Finger press the seams to one side and trim away any overhang at the points. Repeat with the remaining Triangle A's and B's to create 16 sets.

b. Now pin and sew two A/B sets together in the same manner to create half of one Patchwork Square. Repeat with the rest of the A/B sets to make 8 pieces.

c. Pin two halves together, matching the points in the center using a straight pin. Starting at the center point, sew out to one side. Turn the halves over and begin again at the center, sewing out to the side. Press the center seams open. Repeat with the remaining halves to create the remaining 3 Patchwork Squares. See Figure 1 to see how the center block should look.

Attach the Side Panels to Each Patchwork Square

a. Pin two 24" (61 cm) Side Panels to the top and the bottom of each Patchwork Square **right** sides together. Stitch together and press seams toward the Side Panels. Repeat with the other 24" (61 cm) Sides Panels and Squares.

b. Now pin two 31½" (80 cm) Side Panels to the left and right sides of each Patchwork Square and stitch together. Press the seams toward the Side Panels. Repeat for the remaining Side Panels and Squares.

Mount the Patchwork Squares to the Design Foam

Note: Foamology Design Foam is high-density foam designed for home decorating. It comes in different thicknesses and has different options for attaching fabrics. One side has a Sticky Base for easily adhering fabrics to the foam or for attaching the foam directly to your walls. It's easy and quick to cover and mount the foam for fast decorating projects. For this project, you can use the adhesive side against the back of the Patchwork Square and stick the fabric to the foam, or on the other side, where, after centering the Patchwork Square on the non-sticky side, you would wrap the Side Panels around to the adhesive side of the foam and stick. Then you would adhere the foam to the wall. The stick is permanent, so you may want to cover your wall or surface first before sticking. Please follow the manufacturer's instructions and care guide included. We chose to leave the adhesive liner in place and wrap the Side Panels of the Patchwork Square around to the back side of the foam and attach with pins. We then mounted the foam to our wall with small tacks, by nailing the tacks into the wall first and then hanging the foam from them.

a. Center each Patchwork Square onto a square of design foam. Wrap the Side Panels around the sides, folding in the corner neatly (almost like you would a present).

b. Either pin or use the adhesive to attach the fabric to the back of the foam.

c. Mount to your walls as desired.

Dreamweaver Quilt

Finished size: 88" (223.5 cm) x 109.5" (278.1 cm) to fit a Queen bed

Dreamweaver Quilt

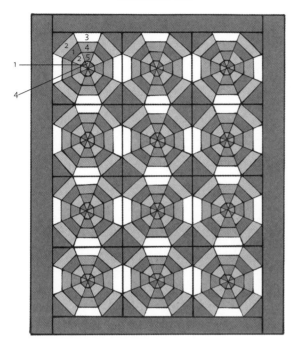

Figure 5

MATERIALS LIST

Fabrics

From 44" (112 cm) wide light- to mid-weight fabric

7½ yards (6.86 m) of Fabric 1 for Patchwork

2½ yards (2.27 m) of Fabric 1 for Borders

3¼ yards (3 m) of Fabric 2 for Patchwork

1⅝ yards (1.49 m) of Fabric 3 for Patchwork

3⅜ yards (3.09 m) of Fabric 4 for Patchwork

1⅝ yards (1.49 m) of Fabric 5 for Patchwork

10 yards (9.14 m) of Fabric 4 for Backing

1 yard (0.91 m) of Fabric 5 for Binding

OTHER SUPPLIES

120" (304.8 cm) x 120" (304.8 cm) extra-loft batting (Fairfield)

2 spools of coordinating all-purpose thread (Coats)

 Cut Out the Pattern Pieces

From the pattern sheet included with this book, cut out:

    Patchwork Triangle A

    Patchwork Triangle B

 Cut Out the Fabric Pieces

Use your rotary cutter, mat, and ruler to cut the specific amounts listed below.

For the Patchwork
From Fabric 1

Cut 16 strips – 6" (15.2 cm) x width of fabric* (wof)

Cut 16 strips – 3½" (8.9 cm) x wof

Cut 16 strips – 4" (10.2 cm) x wof

From Fabric 2

Cut 32 strips – 3½" (8.9 cm) x wof

From Fabric 3

Cut 16 strips – 3½" (8.9 cm) x wof

From Fabric 4

Cut 16 strips – 3½" (8.9 cm) x wof

Cut 16 strips – 4" (10.2 cm) x wof

From Fabric 5

Cut 16 strips – 3½" (8.9 cm) x wof

For the Borders
From Fabric 1

Cut 6 strips – 9" (22.9 cm) x wof for the Side Borders

Cut 5 strips – 7" (17.8 cm) x wof for the Top and Bottom Borders

 Sew the Patchwork Strips

Note: A Strip Set is a set of strips stitched together in the order indicated to make a pieced fabric length.

For Strip Set A

a. On a large, flat surface, lay out three strips of Fabric 1 and two strips of Fabric 2, **right** sides facing up, in the order shown in Figure 2.

Tip: When stitching the strips together, start sewing at alternate ends to avoid the piece getting distorted and curving like a rainbow. Start by pinning the first two fabric strips (9" [22.9 cm] of Fabric 1 and 3½" [8.9 cm] of Fabric 2) **right** sides together, matching the long edges, and stitch. Press the seams in one direction.

b. Pin the third strip (3½" [8.9 cm] of Fabric 1) to the second strip and stitch along the pinned edges. Press the seams in one direction.

c. Continue this process of sewing and pressing the strips to complete the set.

d. Repeat Steps 3a to d fifteen more times to make 16 Strip Set A's.

For Strip Set B

a. On a large, flat surface, lay out strips for Fabrics 3, 4, and 5, **right** sides facing up, from top to bottom in the order shown in Figure 3.

b. Repeat Steps 3b to e for Strip Set A with these fabrics for 16 Strip Set B's, pressing the seam allowances in the opposite direction from Strip Set A.

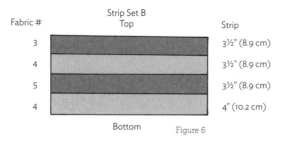

Fabric #	Strip Set B Top	Strip
3		3½" (8.9 cm)
4		3½" (8.9 cm)
5		3½" (8.9 cm)
4		4" (10.2 cm)

Bottom   Figure 6

4   Use the Patterns to Cut Out the Triangles

a. Trace and then cut out 48 Patchwork Triangle A's from the Strip Set A's, matching up the placement lines with the seams on the Strip Sets. You can cut up to 3 Triangle A's from each Strip Set.

b. Trace and then cut out 48 Patchwork Triangle B's from the Strip Set B's, matching up the placement lines with the seams on the Strip Sets. You can cut up to 3 Triangle B's from each Strip Set.

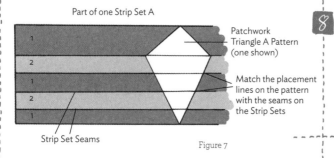

Part of one Strip Set A

Patchwork Triangle A Pattern (one shown)

Match the placement lines on the pattern with the seams on the Strip Sets

Strip Set Seams

Figure 7

5   Sew the Triangles Together to Make the Patchwork Squares

Tip: Finger press* all the seams between the Triangles to keep them from stretching.

a. Pin one Triangle A long edge to one Triangle B long edge, **right** sides together, matching the seams and offsetting the seam allowances. Stitch together, sewing from the point to the wide end of the Triangles. Finger press the seams to one side and trim away any overhang at the points. Repeat with the remaining Triangle A's and B's to create 48 sets.

b. Now pin and sew two A/B sets together in the same manner

to create half of one Patchwork Square. Repeat with the rest of the A/B sets to make 24 squares.

c. Pin two halves together, matching the points in the center using a straight pin. Starting at the center point, sew out to one side. Turn the halves over and begin again at the center, sewing out to the side. Press the center seam open. Repeat with the remaining halves to make twelve 24½" (62.2 cm) Patchwork Squares. See Figure 1 to see how the center block should look.

6   Sew the Patchwork Squares Together

a. Follow the layout in Figure 5 and sew three Patchwork Squares together for each row, matching all the seams. Press the seams to one side, alternating the direction on each row.

b. Sew the four rows together, matching all the seams. Press the seams in one direction.

7   Make and Attach the Borders

a. Sew the 9" (22.9 cm) strips together for the Side Borders to create one long strip and then cut this length into two 109½" (278.1 cm) pieces.

b. Join the 7" (17.8 cm) strips for the Top and Bottom Borders and then cut the length into two 72½" (184.2 cm) pieces.

c. Sew a 7" x 72½" (17.8 x 184.2 cm) strip onto the top and bottom edges of the quilt. Press the seams toward the border.

d. Sew a 9" x 109½" (22.9 x 278.1 cm) strip onto the right and left sides of the quilt. Press the seams toward the border.

e. Turn the Quilt Top **right** side up and press flat.

8   Finish the Quilt

Follow the instructions in the Glossary and Techniques section on Assembling the Quilt* (page 164) and Binding* (page 164).

Pyramid Pillows

Finished sizes: Large – 27" x 28" (68.6 x 71.1 cm); Medium – 23" x 21" (58.4 x 53.3 cm)

These buoyant pillows can be made in two sizes and have a personality all their own with their quirky, modern wonderfulness! Tossed about as comfy throw pillows or prominently placed as modern works of art, they nest perfectly in living rooms and bedrooms for kids of all ages. Vary the mix of prints or solids on either size to suit your mood or room.

NOTES

All seams are ¼" (0.6 cm) unless otherwise stated.

DESIGN INFLUENCE

Triangles

TECHNIQUE USED

Patchwork

Pyramid Pillow Side Layout

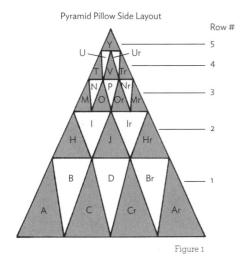

Figure 1

MATERIALS LIST

Large Pillow (scrappy):

Fabrics

From 44" (112 cm) wide (unless scrap dimension given) light-to-mid-weight fabric

¼ yard (0.23 m) solid fabric for Rows 2 and 3

1½ yards (1.37 m) solid fabric for Rows 4, 5, and base

24" x 12½" (61 x 31.8 cm) scraps of 4 different prints for Row 5

21" x 8" (53.3 x 20.3 cm) scraps of 3 different prints for Row 4

12" x 6" (53.3 x 15.2 cm) scraps of 4 different prints for Row 3

10½" x 5½" (27.7 x 14 cm) scraps of 3 different prints for Row 2

12" x 4½" (30.5 x 11.4 cm) scrap of print for Row 1

2 yards (1.83 m) of muslin for pillow form

OTHER SUPPLIES

72" x 90" (182.9 x 228.6 cm) twin-size cotton batting (Fairfield)

36 ounces (1.02 kg) of fiberfill (Fairfield) or three 12-ounce (0.34-kg) bags of Nature-Fil Blend by Fairfield

1 spool coordinating all-purpose thread (Coats)

16" (40.6 cm) diameter bouncy ball (we found ours at Five Below)

Medium Pillow (2 colors):

Fabrics

From 44" (112 cm) wide light- to mid-weight fabric

1⅛ yards (1 m) of print 1 for pieced sides

1⅛ yards (1 m) of print 2 for pieced sides and base

1¾ yards (1.6 m) of muslin for pillow form

OTHER SUPPLIES

45" x 60" (114.3 x 125.4 cm) crib-size cotton batting (Fairfield)

24 ounces (0.68 kg) of fiberfill or two 12-ounce (0.34-kg) bags Nature-Fil Blend by Fairfield

1 spool of coordinating all-purpose thread (Coats)

12" (30.5 cm) diameter bouncy ball (we found ours at Five Below)

ADDITIONAL TOOLS NEEDED

Yardstick

24" (61 cm) long rotary cutting ruler

Turning tool

Temporary fabric adhesive (505 Spray & Fix Temporary Fabric Adhesive)

Hand-sewing needle

 Cut Out the Pattern Pieces

From the pattern sheet included with this book, cut out:

Large Pyramid Triangle Pieces A to Y

Medium Pyramid Triangle Pieces A to Y

 Cut Out the Fabric Pieces

Note: A ¼" (0.6 cm) seam allowance is included on all of the pattern pieces. Trace the pattern pieces onto the **right** side of the fabrics. For the pieces marked with an "r" in Figure 1, turn the pattern over to trace the reverse side onto the fabric.

Large Pillow

From the solid fabric for Rows 2 and 3, cut three of each:
Large Pyramid Pillow Piece N
Large Pyramid Pillow Piece P
Large Pyramid Pillow Piece Nr
Large Pyramid Pillow Piece U
Large Pyramid Pillow Piece Ur

From the solid fabric for Rows 4 and 5 and the Pillow Base:
For the Pillow Base: Use your chalk pencil and yardstick and mark directly onto the **wrong** side of the fabric. Draw a 27" (68.6 cm) line parallel to and 1" (2.5 cm) from one selvage (Line A). Mark the center of this line. From this center mark, draw a 23½" (59.7 cm) long line (Line B) perpendicular to the first line. Place the 27" (68.6 cm) mark of the yardstick at one end of Line A and the 0 mark at the end of Line B. Draw a line connecting the two points. Draw another line connecting the other end of Line A to the end of Line B in the same manner to form a triangle for the Base Panel. Add ¼" (0.6 cm) seam allowance around the triangle. Cut out the Pillow Base. (See Figure 2.)

Draw the Pillow Base

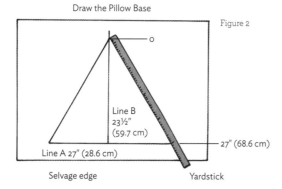

Figure 2

Line B 23½" (59.7 cm)

Line A 27" (28.6 cm)

27" (68.6 cm)

Selvage edge

Yardstick

From the same fabric, cut 3 of each of the following pattern pieces:
Large Pyramid Pillow Piece B
Large Pyramid Pillow Piece D
Large Pyramid Pillow Piece Br
Large Pyramid Pillow Piece I
Large Pyramid Pillow Piece Ir

From the first 24" x 12½" (61 x 31.8 cm) scrap
Cut 3 of the Large Pyramid Pillow Piece A

From the second 24" x 12½" (61 x 31.8 cm) scrap
Cut 3 of the Large Pyramid Pillow Piece C

From the third 24" x 12½" (61 x 31.8 cm) scrap
Cut 3 of the Large Pyramid Pillow Piece Cr

From the fourth 24" x 12½" (61 x 31.8 cm) scrap
Cut 3 of the Large Pyramid Pillow Piece Ar

From the first 21" x 8" (53.3 x 20.3 cm) scrap
Cut 3 of the Large Pyramid Pillow Piece H

From the second 21" x 8" (53.3 x 20.3 cm) scrap
Cut 3 of the Large Pyramid Pillow Piece J

From the third 21" x 8" (53.3 x 20.3 cm) scrap
Cut 3 of the Large Pyramid Pillow Piece Hr

From the first 12" x 6" (30.5 x 15.2 cm) scrap
Cut 3 of the Large Pyramid Pillow Piece M

From the second 12" x 6" (30.5 x 15.2 cm) scrap
Cut 3 of the Large Pyramid Pillow Piece O

From the third 12" x 6" (30.5 x 15.2 cm) scrap
Cut 3 of the Large Pyramid Pillow Piece Or

From the fourth 12" x 6" (30.5 x 15.2 cm) scrap
Cut 3 of the Large Pyramid Pillow Piece Mr

From the first 10½" x 5½" (26.7 x 14 cm) scrap
Cut 3 of the Large Pyramid Pillow Piece T

From the second 10½" x 5½" (26.7 x 14 cm) scrap
Cut 3 of the Large Pyramid Pillow Piece V

From the third 10½" x 5½" (26.7 x 14 cm) scrap
Cut 3 of the Large Pyramid Pillow Piece Tr

From the 12" x 4½" (30.5 x 11.4 cm) scrap
Cut 3 of the Large Pyramid Pillow Piece Y

Muslin
Note: The muslin will be used to create the Pillow Form Base and Pillow Form Sides in Step 4.

For the Pillow Form Base: Lay the muslin open in front of you on a large, flat surface. Use your chalk pencil and yardstick and mark directly on the fabric. Starting in one corner of the fabric, draw a 13½" (34.3 cm) line parallel to and 1" (2.5 cm) from one selvage (Line A). From one end, draw a 23½" (59.7 cm) long line (Line B) perpendicular to the first line. Use the yardstick to draw a 27" (68.6 cm) line connecting Lines A and B to complete the triangle to form the Pillow Form Base Panel. Now, using the rotary cutting ruler draw a ½" (1.3 cm) seam allowance around the outside of the Base Triangle. Cut along the seam allowance line, then flip this first Panel and use it as a template to cut a second Pillow Form Base Panel right next to where you cut the first panel. Set aside the remaining muslin to use for cutting out the Pillow Form Sides in Step 4. (See Figure 3.)

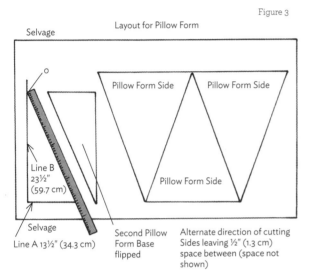

Figure 3

Layout for Pillow Form

Medium Pillow

From Print 1, cut 3 of each of the following pattern pieces:

Medium Pyramid Pillow Piece A
Medium Pyramid Pillow Piece C
Medium Pyramid Pillow Piece Cr
Medium Pyramid Pillow Piece Ar
Medium Pyramid Pillow Piece H
Medium Pyramid Pillow Piece J
Medium Pyramid Pillow Piece Hr
Medium Pyramid Pillow Piece M
Medium Pyramid Pillow Piece O
Medium Pyramid Pillow Piece Or
Medium Pyramid Pillow Piece Mr
Medium Pyramid Pillow Piece T
Medium Pyramid Pillow Piece V
Medium Pyramid Pillow Piece Tr
Medium Pyramid Pillow Piece Y

From Print 2

For the Pillow Base: Refer to Figure 2 as a guide and use your chalk pencil and yardstick and mark directly onto the **wrong** side of the fabric. Draw a 23" (58.4 cm) line parallel to and 1" (2.5 cm) from one selvage (Line A). Mark the center of this line. From this center mark, draw a 20" (50.8 cm) long line (Line B) perpendicular to the first line. Place the 23" (58.4 cm) mark of the yardstick at one end of Line A and the 0 mark at the end of Line B. Draw a line connecting the two points. Draw another line connecting the other end of Line A to the end of Line B in the same manner to form a triangle for the Base Panel. Add ¼" (0.6 cm) seam allowance around the triangle. Cut out the Pillow Base.

Cut 3 of each of the following pattern pieces:

Medium Pyramid Pillow Piece B
Medium Pyramid Pillow Piece D
Medium Pyramid Pillow Piece Br
Medium Pyramid Pillow Piece I
Medium Pyramid Pillow Piece Ir
Medium Pyramid Pillow Piece N
Medium Pyramid Pillow Piece P
Medium Pyramid Pillow Piece Nr
Medium Pyramid Pillow Piece U
Medium Pyramid Pillow Piece Ur

Muslin

For the Pillow Form Base: Refer to Figure 3 as a guide and lay the muslin open in front of you on a large, flat surface. Use your chalk pencil and yardstick and mark directly onto the fabric. Starting in one corner of the fabric, draw an 11½" (29.2 cm) line parallel to and 1" (2.5 cm) from one selvage edge (Line A). From one end, draw a 20" (50.8 cm) long line (Line B) perpendicular to the first line. Use the yardstick to draw a 23" (58.4) line connecting Lines A and B to complete the triangle and form the Pillow Form Base Panel. Now, using the rotary cutting ruler, draw a ½" (1.3 cm) seam allowance around the outside of the Base Triangle. Cut along the seam allowance line and then use this first Panel to cut a second Pillow Form Base Panel, flipping the panel as shown in Figure 3. Set aside the remaining muslin to use for cutting out the Pillow Form Sides in Step 4.

Make the Pieced Pyramid Sides

Note: The instructions for the construction of the Large and Medium Pyramid Pillows are the same.

a. On a flat surface, lay out one of each Template piece in the rows shown in the layout. (See Figure 1.)

b. Align the first two pieces of a row along the long edges, with **right** sides together and stitch. Press seam allowance open. Continue in this manner until all pieces of a row are sewn together. Then sew each of the other rows together. Tip: When a triangle point is completed, check to ensure there is a ¼" (0.6 cm) seam allowance below or above the point. If there is not, adjust the previously sewn seam.

c. Align the top of Row 1 with the bottom of Row 2, with **right** sides together, matching and pinning the triangle points where necessary. (See Figure 1.) Sew these rows together and press the seam allowances open. Continue in this manner until all rows are sewn together to form one Pieced Pyramid Side.

d. Repeat the Steps 3a to 3c to construct two more Pieced Pyramid Sides.

4 Cut the Pillow Form, Muslin, and Batting Pieces

a. Using one of the completed Pieced Pyramid Sides as a template and your chalk pencil, mark 3 Pillow Form Side Panels onto a single layer of the muslin, alternating directions and leaving a ½" (1.3 cm) space in between. (See Figure 3.) Add an additional ¼" (0.6 cm) seam allowance around each panel. Cut along these drawn lines for 3 Pillow Form Side Panels.

b. Using the Muslin Pillow Form Side and Base Panels, cut from the batting:
Pillow Form Side Panels
Pillow Form Base Panels

5 Make the Pieced Pillow Cover

a. Align two Pieced Pyramid Side Panels along one long side, **right** sides together, and pin, ensuring the triangle points match. Sew the pinned edge together, starting and stopping ¼" (0.6 cm) from each end. Press the seam allowance open.

b. Attach the third Pieced Pyramid Side Panel to the other two in the same way to form the pyramid.

c. Find and mark the center of one side of the Base Panel. Pin this marked side, **right** sides together, to the base of one of the Side Panels, matching the center points. Sew the pinned edge together, starting and stopping ¼" (0.6 cm) from each end. Press the seam allowance open. Note: The points of the Base Panel will extend past the edges of the Side Panel.

d. Turn the Pillow Cover **right** side out, use a turning tool* to gently push out the top point.

e. Fold and press the remaining raw edges of the Base Panel and the bottoms of the two Side Panels under ¼" (0.6 cm).

6 Make the Pillow Form

a. Using temporary adhesive spray, attach one batting Pillow Form Panel to each muslin Pillow Form Panel. Note: Attach the batting to one muslin Base Panel first, and then ensure the second Base Panel is the reverse of the first when attaching the batting. The muslin/batting panels will be considered as a single panel in the following instructions.

b. Place the two Pillow Form Base Panels, **right** sides together, matching the Line B edges, and pin. Sew a ½" (1.3 cm) seam 1" (2.5 cm) long from each end, leaving a large opening in the center. Press the seam allowance open along the entire length of Line B.

c. Align two Pillow Form Side Panels along one long side, **right** sides together, and pin. Sew a ½" (1.3 cm) seam along the pinned edge, starting and stopping ½" (1.3 cm) from each end. Press the seam allowance open.

d. In the same manner, attach the third Pillow Form Side Panel to the other two to form the pyramid.

e. Using the procedure in Step 5c, attach the Pillow Form Base to the bottom of each of the Side Panels. The only difference is that you will use a ½" (1.3 cm) seam allowance and start and stop ½" (1.3 cm) from each end.

f. Turn the Pillow Form **right** side out through the opening in the center of the Base. Use a turning tool to gently push out the points.

g. Firmly stuff the top point of the pillow with fiberfill to about one-quarter of the way down the pyramid. Insert the ball into the Pillow Form and then continue stuffing from the bottom points around the ball, keeping the ball in the center of the Pillow Form. Note: This gives the form a hard center as well as the softness of stuffing.

h. Match the folded edges of the opening in the base, and, using a threaded hand-sewing needle, slipstitch* the opening closed.

7 Finish the Pyramid Pillow

a. Insert the Pillow Form into the Pieced Pillow Cover, ensuring the top point of the cover is filled.

b. Align the base over the form, matching the folded edges of the base with the pieced side folded edges, and pin. Slipstitch the bottom base closed.

Cozy Patch Floor Cushions

Finished size: 30" (76.2 cm) square

Simple, bold patchwork shapes provide the perfect platform for your favorite prints.
These cushions also make themselves at home wherever they're tossed,
offering up a comfy spot to rest and relax.

NOTES
All seams are ½" (1.3 cm) unless otherwise stated.

DESIGN INFLUENCE
Triangles

TECHNIQUE USED
Patchwork

Figure 1

Pillow Front

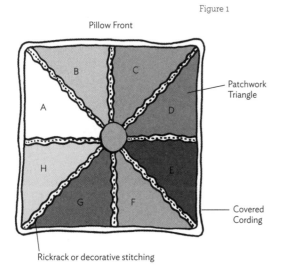

Rickrack or decorative stitching

— Patchwork Triangle

— Covered Cording

MATERIALS LIST

Fabrics
From 44" wide (112 cm) light- to mid-weight fabric
8 fat quarters (or ½ yard [0.45 m] each of 8 fabrics) for Pillow Front
1⅝ yards (1.49 m) of coordinating solid or print for Back and cording
  covering

OTHER SUPPLIES
3⅝ yards (3.31 m) cotton filler cord (size ¹²⁄₃₂" [0.95 cm] – Wrights)
1 yard (0.91 m) of 20" (50.8 cm) wide tear-away stabilizer, cut into 1"
(2.5 cm) strips (Pellon 806 Stitch-n-Tear)

2 buttons for covering – size 2½" (6.4 cm) Dritz (please save the
  instructions and template on the back of the package)
30" (76.2 cm) pillow form (Fairfield)
1 spool of coordinating all-purpose thread (Coats)
1 spool of coordinating all-purpose or embroidery thread for decorative stitching (the decorative stitch we used was from Janome
  Memory Craft 6500 – mode 3 utility #28)
or
2 packages of ½" (1.3 cm) wide rickrack in a contrasting color –
  optional (Wrights)
1 spool of coordinating button and carpet thread (Coats)
1 long doll needle, 5" (12.7 cm) (Prym-Dritz 2 Piece Doll Needles)

ADDITIONAL TOOLS NEEDED
1 sheet of paper measuring 17" x 17" (43.2 cm x 43.2 cm) and a pencil
24" (61 cm) ruler
Masking tape and marker
Decorative stitching foot
Zipper/cording foot (for your sewing machine)
1 standard hand-sewing needle

 Draw and Cut Out the Patchwork Triangle Pattern Piece
  a. Using a ruler and pencil, measure and mark the
    dimensions below directly onto the paper.
  b. Draw a line 15" (38.1 cm) long about 1" (2.5 cm) from one
    edge of the paper.
  c. Using one end of this line as a starting point, draw another
    15" (38.1 cm) long line perpendicular to the first line.
  d. Draw a diagonal line connecting the two ends.
  e. Add a ½" (1.3 cm) seam allowance to all sides.
  f. Cut along the seam allowance lines for the Patchwork
    Triangle Pattern. Mark one side as the **right** side.

2. Cut Out the Fabric Pieces
Using Figure 1 as a guide, arrange your fabrics as desired and
  label them A to H using a marker and masking tape.

Triangle Fabrics

For fabrics A, C, E, and G, cut 1 triangle each with the **right** side of the Triangle Patchwork Pattern piece facing up.

For fabrics B, D, F, and H, cut 1 triangle each with the **wrong** side of the Triangle Patchwork Pattern piece facing up.

Pillow Back

Cut a 31" (78.7 cm) square near one corner of the coordinating fabric.

Cording

Fold the remaining coordinating fabric on the bias*. Use your rotary cutter, mat, and ruler to cut enough 2⅛" (5.4 cm) wide strips on the bias to create a 130" (330.2 cm) long strip when sewn together.

Buttons

Cut 2 button circles from your choice of fabric using the template from the back of the button package.

 Make the Pillow Front

a. Lay the triangle pieces out in front of you in an order that is pleasing to you, using the diagram as a guide.

b. Pin and sew the triangles together in pairs along the diagonal edges. Press the seam allowances open. Trim away the overhanging points. You will now have four squares.

c. Lay squares in two rows of two with all of the diagonal seams meeting in the center. Pin and sew the squares into two rows, matching the diagonal seams. Press the seam allowances open.

d. Sew the two rows together, matching the center and diagonal seams. Press seam allowances open.

4 Embellish the Pillow Front

Whether you choose to adorn your pillow with rickrack or decorative stitching, here are some guidelines:

For decorative stitching: Pin the 1" (2.5 cm) stabilizer strips to the seams on the **wrong** side of the Pillow Front. Thread your machine with the coordinating or embroidery thread for the decorative stitching. Stitch along each of the diagonal seams, sewing from the center point to the outside edge. Carefully remove or trim the excess stabilizer away from the stitching. Note: The stitch we used was a "satin zigzag," a zigzag stitch where the needle goes through the same hole more than once.

For the rickrack trim: Pin the rickrack to the **right** side of the Pillow Front, centering it along each of the diagonal seams.

Thread your machine with coordinating thread. Stitch a straight stitch along the center of the rickrack.

 Cover the Cording and Attach It to the Pillow Front

a. To sew the bias strips together into one long continuous piece, start by placing two strips perpendicular to each other, matching the two short ends, with **right** sides together, and pin them in place. Stitch a ¼" (0.6 cm) seam across the pinned edge. Press the seam allowances open. Repeat until you've sewn all of the bias strips into one long strip measuring 130" (330.2 cm).

b. Fold this bias strip in half the long way with **right** side out, capturing the cording in the middle as you go and pinning the long edges together. Use your zipper/cording foot and stitch a ⅜" (1 cm) seam from the matched edges to hold them in place.

c. Position one end of the cording at the bottom center of the **right** side of the Pillow Front. Matching the raw edges, ease and pin the cording around the Pillow Front, clipping* the seam allowance of the cord covering at the corners, being careful not to clip through the stitching. Cut off the extra cording 1" (2.5 cm) past the first end.

d. Begin sewing 2" (5.1 cm) in from one cording end and stitch around the pinned edges. Stop sewing 5" (12.7 cm) from where you started. On the cut end of your cording, use your seam ripper, and remove 3" (7.6 cm) of stitching from the covering, pulling it back away from the cording. Overlap the exposed cording with the first end and cut across both where they meet, so there is no overlap.

e. Fold and press the short end of the covering ¼" (0.6 cm) under toward the **wrong** side. Wrap it around the first end of the cording, enclosing the cut ends. Pin the edges of the cover together, then pin them to the edge of the Pillow Front. Finish stitching the covered cording in place.

 Sew the Back and Front of the Pillow Together

Note: Continue to use the zipper/cording foot to accommodate the cording.

a. Find the center point of the Pillow Back and make a mark on the **right** side with your chalk pencil. This will help when sewing the buttons to the pillow in Step 7.

b. With the **right** sides together, pin the Pillow Back to the Pillow Front, matching all edges and corners.

c. Using the zipper/cording foot on your machine, sew the Back to the Front, leaving a 20" (50.8 cm) opening on one side. Trim the corners*, being careful not to cut the stitching.

d. Turn the cover **right** side out, gently pushing out the corners and cording with a turning tool and press.

e. Insert the pillow form through the opening in the cover.

f. Fold and press each side of the opening ½" (1.3 cm) under and pin the edges together. With a threaded hand-sewing needle, slipstitch* along the pinned edges to close the opening in the pillow.

 Attach the Buttons to the Pillow

a. Following the manufacturer's instructions, cover the buttons using the fabric circles you cut in Step 2.

b. Place the first button on the **right** side of the Pillow Front, being sure to cover the center point where all of the triangle sections meet. Use the 5" (12.7 cm) long needle and about 30" (76.2 cm) of the button and carpet thread to hand sew the button through the pillow to the marked center of the Pillow Back. Attach the second button to the back and continue to sew both buttons securely in place, pulling the threads tightly in order to tuft the cushion.

Improv Pillows

Finished size: 22" (55.9 cm) square

Quilted for extra softness and comfort, these modern patch pillows will keep your style fresh.
Two different design ideas give you just the right launchpad for your unique and intuitive creations!

Improvising on the Log Cabin technique, the center blocks of these pillows are made up of various brightly colored prints I had in my studio offset in a frame of white borders. I created the centers following the traditional Log Cabin blueprint of building strips around a center block, but I modified it by playing with the different widths of the strips as well as the direction I sewed them in. It's very easy and fun to do, and I have provided some guidelines for how to create your own. This is a freeform project, so you cannot go wrong. Have fun with the colors and experiment.

NOTES

All seams are ¼" (0.6 cm) unless otherwise stated. The seam allowance is included in all pattern pieces and measurements. Press seam allowances to one side except where noted.

DESIGN INFLUENCE

Improv Log Cabin

TECHNIQUE USED

Patchwork

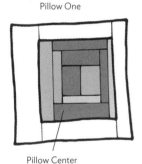
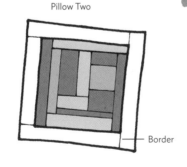

Figure 1

Pillow One

Pillow Two

Pillow Center

Border

MATERIALS LIST

Fabrics

From 44" (112 cm) wide light- to mid-weight fabric

2 to 2½ yards (1.83 to 2.27 m) total of different, brightly colored fabric scraps for the Pillow Centers (may include scrap fabrics, leftover prints, fat quarters, or ⅛ yard [0.11 m] cuts of fabrics)

1⅜ yards (1.26 m) of solid white for the Borders

1½ yards (1.37 m) of solid for the Backing

1½ yards (1.37 m) of muslin for the backing of patchwork panels

OTHER SUPPLIES

45" x 60" (114.3 x 152.4 cm) Poly-fil Extra-Loft quilt batting (Fairfield)

Two 22" (55.9 cm) pillow forms (Fairfield)

1 spool of coordinating all-purpose thread (Coats)

1 spool of transparent thread (Coats)

ADDITIONAL TOOLS NEEDED

1 package of large safety pins

Walking foot (for your sewing machine)

Turning tool (Prym-Dritz)

1 standard hand-sewing needle

Cut Out the Fabrics

Use your rotary cutter, mat, and ruler for the following:

Border Fabric

For Pillow One:

Cut 1 Top Border strip: 7" (17.8 cm) x width of fabric (wof)

Cut 1 Bottom Border strip: 5" (12.7 cm) x wof

Cut 1 Right Side Border strip: 6" (15.2 cm) x wof

Cut 1 Left Side Border strip: 5½" (14 cm) x wof

For Pillow Two:

Cut 1 Top Border strip: 4" (10.2 cm) x width of fabric (wof)

Cut 1 Bottom Border strip: 5" (12.7 cm) x wof

Cut 1 Right Side Border strip: 4" (10.2 cm) x wof

Cut 1 Left Side Border strip: 8" (20.3 cm) x wof

Backing Fabric

Cut 2 pieces – 23" (58.4 cm) square

Muslin
Cut 2 pieces – 25" (63.5 cm) square

Batting
Cut 2 pieces – 25" (63.5 cm) square

Design and Make the Pillow Center
To make the Pillow Centers:

You can lay out your pieces ahead of time and play with your composition, or you can just add pieces as you go, choosing whichever fabric seems to work next. Strips can be pieced from multiple fabrics. (See Figure 1.)

Angled seams can be easily made by laying two strips **right** side up on a cutting mat, overlapping the long edges that will be sewn by about 3" (7.6 cm). Using a ruler, rotary cutter, and mat, make an angled cut across the overlapped area. Then pin and sew them **right** sides together, matching the angled edges. Discard the trimmed pieces, or use them in a different part of the pillow.

a. Start by cutting a square or rectangle from your first fabric to be your center piece.

b. Find a fabric similar in size and sew it to the center piece. Square up* your two pieces and press.

c. Continue sewing additional strips and blocks to these center pieces, squaring and pressing your block as you go. Keep your rotary cutter, mat, and ruler close by to trim or square up any ends or overhanging edges.

d. Continue to build onto your Pillow Centers until they reach these sizes when they are squared up: Pillow One – 14" (35.6 cm) high x 14½" (36.8 cm) wide; Pillow Two – 17" (43.2 cm) high x 14" (35.6 cm) wide.

Add the Border Fabrics
a. Cut off the selvages* from all of the border strips.

b. For either pillow, sew the Left and Right Borders to the Pillow Center. Use your rotary cutter, mat, and ruler to trim off the excess and square the pillow to the center piece.

c. Sew the Top and Bottom Borders to the Pillow Front. Trim off the excess to make a 25" (63.5 cm) square.

Machine Quilt the Pillow Fronts
a. For either pillow, lay one piece of muslin on a flat surface and smooth out any wrinkles.

b. Place one piece of batting onto the muslin.

c. Lay the Pillow Front **right** side up on the top of the batting, creating a sandwich of the muslin, batting, and Pillow Front, and smooth out the wrinkles.

d. Use safety pins to pin the layers together every 4" (10.2 cm) to secure the layers in place.

e. Attach the walking foot to your machine and thread your needle with transparent thread. Carefully stitch-in-the-ditch* along the seams of the Pillow Front, starting in the center and working out to the sides.

f. Square up the Pillow Front to a 23" (58.4 cm) square by trimming off the excess batting, muslin, and borders.

Complete the Pillow
a. For either pillow, with the **right** sides together pin the Pillow Back to the Pillow Front, matching all edges and corners.

b. Sew the Pillow Back to the Front, using a ½" (1.3 cm) seam allowance, pivoting* around each corner and leaving an 18" (45.7 cm) opening on one side. Trim the corners*, being careful not to cut the stitching.

c. Turn the cover **right** side out, gently pushing out the corners with a turning tool*, then press the edges flat.

d. Insert the pillow form through the opening in the cover.

e. Fold each side of the opening under ½" (1.3 cm) and pin the folded edges together. Using a hand-sewing needle and thread, slipstitch* along the pinned edges to close the opening in the pillow.

In the Moment Quilt

Finished size: 66" (167.6 cm) wide x 84" (213.4 cm) long (Twin)

Colorful, comfy, and spirited! Enjoy the warmth and beauty of your improvisational masterpiece wherever you are.
It's equally at home as a sweet quilted cover for bed or couch, on the wall as a statement piece
for bedroom and living room, or on the go as an extra special picnic blanket.

NOTES

All seams are ¼" (0.6 cm) unless otherwise stated. The seam
allowance is included in all pattern pieces and measurements.
Press seam allowances to one side except where noted.

DESIGN INFLUENCE

Improv Log Cabin

TECHNIQUE USED

Patchwork

Figure 1

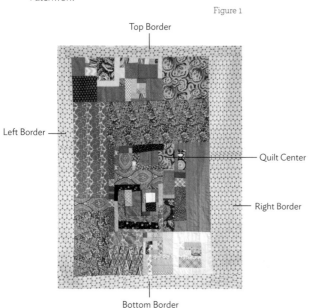

Top Border

Left Border

Quilt Center

Right Border

Bottom Border

MATERIALS LIST

Fabrics

From 44" (112 cm) wide light- to mid-weight fabric
5 to 6 yards (4.57 to 5.49 m) total of fabric scraps for the Quilt Center
(this can include leftover quilt blocks, solids, small prints, and larger
pieces of large-scale prints in cottons and cotton blends)
2¼ yards (2.06 m) of coordinating print for Border

5 yards (4.57 m) of coordinating solid or print for Backing
⅝ yard (0.57 m) of coordinating solid or print for Binding

OTHER SUPPLIES

72" x 96" (182.9 x 243.8 cm) piece of low-loft batting
(Twin – Fairfield)
2 spools of coordinating all-purpose thread (Coats)

ADDITIONAL TOOLS NEEDED

Large safety pins
1 standard hand-sewing needle

 Cut Borders, Backing, and Binding Fabrics

Use your rotary cutter, mat, and ruler for the following.

Border Fabric

Cut 2 Top Border Strips – 4½" (11.4 cm) x width of fabric* (wof)
Cut 2 Bottom Border Strips – 5¾" (14.6 cm) x wof
Cut 3 Left Border Strips – 6" (15.2 cm) x wof
Cut 3 Right Border Strips – 13" (33 cm) x wof

Backing Fabric

Cut 2 panels – 90" (228.6 cm) long x wof

Binding Fabric

Cut 8 strips – 2½" (6.4 cm) x wof

 Design and Make the Quilt Center

Inspired by the technique of improvisational patchwork, I
created the center design of this quilt without any pattern.
It is made up of various strips and blocks of fabric from my
studio that were scraps from previous projects I worked
on. I sewed these together along with some vintage fabrics
I had been saving to make this very random but personal
mix of patchwork. It is easy and fun to do and I have
provided some guidelines for how to make your own! (See
Figure 1.)

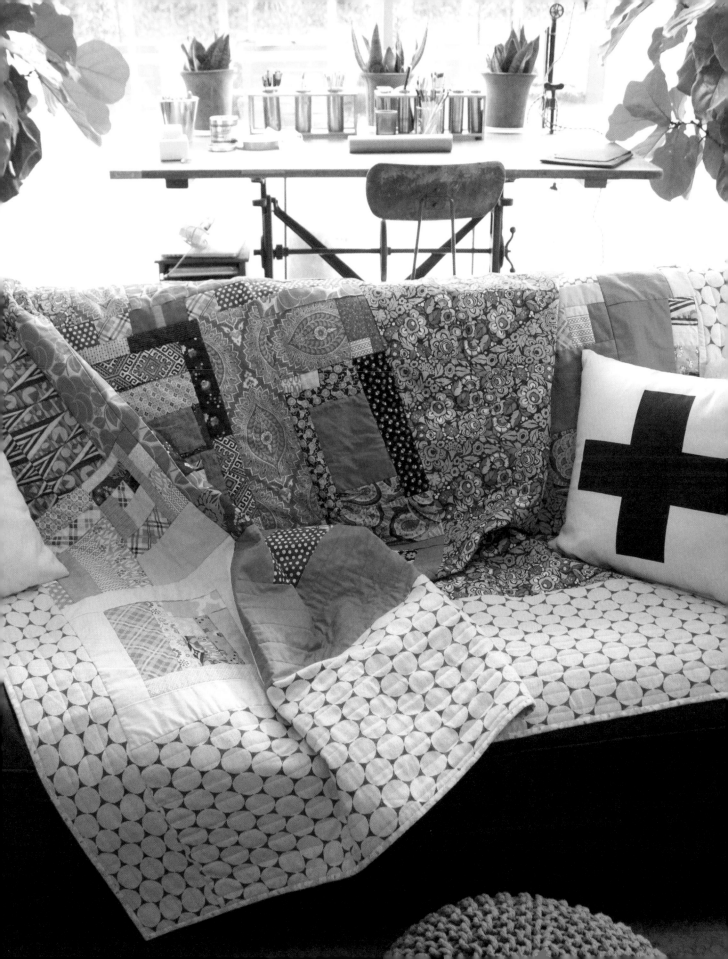

Follow These Guidelines and Techniques When Creating the Quilt Center:

- This is a freeform project, so you cannot go wrong.

- Have fun with the colors and experiment. Use accent fabrics in small amounts to give your quilt a pop of color.

- Cut the largest pieces of fabric you have first. You can use the scraps from them in other areas of the quilt.

- Lay out these large pieces and other fabrics you wish to feature on a flat surface and play with their composition. You can cut smaller pieces to fill in blank spaces.

- Fill strips can be pieced from multiple fabrics.

- Once the fabrics and blocks are laid out in a pleasing arrangement, measure and trim the pieces being sewn together to equal lengths and then sew these pieces together.

- Sew the pieces together from smallest to largest, pressing as you go.

- Keep your rotary cutter, mat, and ruler close by to trim or square up* any ends or overhanging edges.

- Angled seams can be easily made by laying two strips **right** side up on a cutting mat, overlapping the long edges that will be sewn by about 3" (7.6 cm). Using a ruler, mat, and rotary cutter, make an angled cut across the overlapped area. Then pin and sew the **right** sides together, matching the angled edges. Discard the trimmed pieces, or use them in a different part of the quilt top.

- Avoid matching seams in the design; keep it fun and organic.

- Continue to build onto your Quilt Center until the size is 48" (121.9 cm) wide x 74¾" (190 cm) long.

- Follow the directions in the Glossary and Techniques section (page 168) to square up the Quilt Center before adding the Borders.

3 Add the Borders to the Quilt Center

a. Cut the selvages* from the Left Border strips. Sew the strips together along the short ends, **right** sides together, to make one long strip. Trim this strip to 74¾" (190 cm) long. Sew the border to the left side edge of the Quilt Center and press.

b. Repeat Step 3a to attach the Right Border to the **right** side edge of the Quilt Center.

c. Repeat Step 3a for the Top and Bottom Borders, but trim each of those strips to 66" (167.6 cm).

4 Finish the Quilt

Follow the instructions in the Glossary and Techniques section (page 164) on Assembling the Quilt and Binding*.

Wanderlust Quilt

Finished size: 64¾" (164.5 cm) wide x 84" (213.4 cm) long (Twin)

Bring a touch of the exotic into your home with this lush, colorful, stripy quilt made with vintage sari silks. Warm and luxurious, it makes a lovely gift for a special friend.

NOTES

All seams are ¼" (0.6 cm) unless otherwise stated. The seam allowance is included in all measurements. Press all seam allowances to one side as you sew.

DESIGN INFLUENCE

Stripes

TECHNIQUE USED

Patchwork

Figure 1

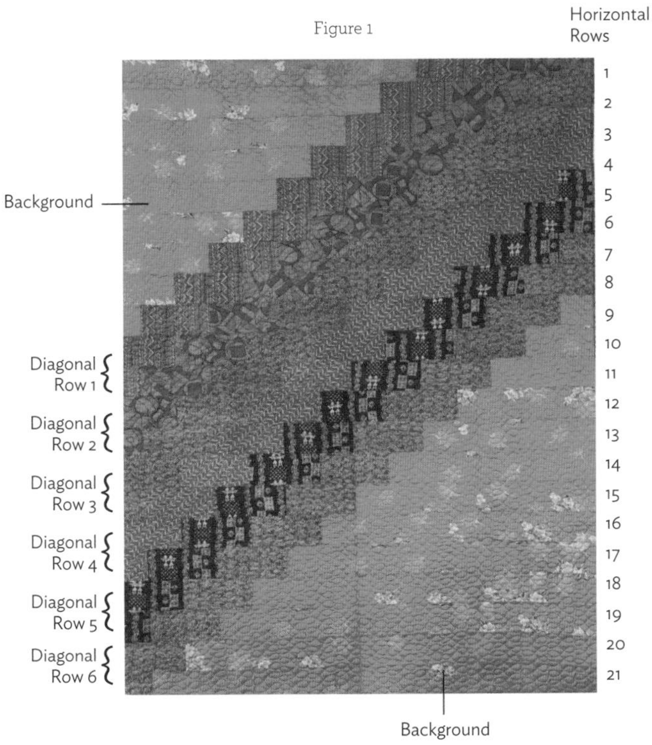

Horizontal Rows: 1–21 labeled on the right side. Background labeled at top left and bottom center. Diagonal Row 1 through Diagonal Row 6 labeled on the left side.

MATERIALS LIST

Note: For this quilt I used recycled silk saris, which measured 5 yards (4.57 m) long and 45" (114 cm) wide. I did not use the entire amount of fabric from all of the saris, but instead cut the amount I needed from the full length, and reserved the remain-ing fabric for other projects. You can use the same measurements listed with another similar lightweight, silky fabric in place of the sari prints. The yardage is listed following.

Fabrics

From 45" (114 cm) wide lightweight sari or silky fabric (unless otherwise noted)

2⅝ yards (2.45 m) of sari or silky print for Background

3½ yards (3.2 m) of sari or silky print 1 for Diagonal Rows 1 and 4 and Backing

3¼ yards (3 m) of sari or silky print 2 for Diagonal Row 2 and Backing

1⅛ yards (1 m) of sari or silky print 3 for Diagonal Rows 3 and 6

⅝ yard (0.62 m) of sari or silky print 4 for Diagonal Row 5

10⅛ yards (9.26 m) of 45" (114 cm) wide muslin for Underlining of Quilt Top and Backing

⅝ yard (0.62 m) of sari or silky print 5 for Binding

OTHER SUPPLIES

72" x 96" (183 x 246.8 cm) piece of silk batting (Hobbs)

2 large spools of coordinating all-purpose thread (Coats)

Fine silk straight pins (Prym Dritz)

Sizing spray

Temporary fabric adhesive (505 Spray and Fix Temporary Fabric Adhesive)

ADDITIONAL TOOLS NEEDED

Masking tape and marker

1 standard hand-sewing needle

1 Cut Out the Fabric Pieces

Use your rotary cutter, mat, and ruler to cut the specific amounts listed following. Use a piece of masking tape and a marker to label the groups of sub-strips as you cut them.

Tip: The silky fabric of the saris tends to move around when cutting. Instead of sliding the ruler across the fabric, lift and place it as you measure and cut the fabric.

Quilt Top

From Background Print

Cut 17 strips: 4¾" (12.1 cm) x width of fabric* (wof)

From these 17 strips cut:

2 pieces A – 4¾" (12.1 cm) wide x 5⅜" (13.7 cm) long
3 pieces B – 4¾" (12.1 cm) wide x 10" (25.4 cm) long
3 pieces C – 4¾" (12.1 cm) wide x 14⅝" (37.1 cm) long
3 pieces D – 4¾" (12.1 cm) wide x 19¼" (48.9 cm) long
3 pieces E – 4¾" (12.1 cm) wide x 23⅞" (60.6 cm) long
2 pieces F – 4¾" (12.1 cm) wide x 28½" (72.4 cm) long
2 pieces G – 4¾" (12.1 cm) wide x 33⅛" (84.1 cm) long
6 pieces H – 4¾" (12.1 cm) wide x 37¾" (95.9 cm) long
2 pieces I – 4¾" (12.1 cm) wide x 42⅜" (107.6 cm) long

From Sari Print 1

Cut 6 strips – 4¾" (12.1 cm) x wof

From these 6 strips cut:

3 pieces A – 4¾" (12.1 cm) wide x 5⅜" (13.7 cm) long
22 pieces B – 4¾" (12.1 cm) wide x 10" (25.4 cm) long

From Sari Print 2

Cut 4 strips – 4¾" (12.1 cm) x wof

From these 4 strips cut:

1 piece A – 4¾" (12.1 cm) wide x 5⅜" (13.7 cm) long
12 pieces B – 4¾" (12.1 cm) wide x 10" (25.4 cm) long

From Sari Print 3

Cut 8 strips – 4¾" (12.1 cm) x wof

From these 8 strips cut:

4 pieces A – 4¾" (12.1 cm) wide x 5⅜" (13.7 cm) long
26 pieces B – 4¾" (12.1 cm) wide x 10" (25.4 cm) long

From Sari Print 4

Cut 4 strips 4¾" (12.1 cm) x wof

From these 4 strips cut:

2 pieces A – 4¾" (12.1 cm) wide x 5⅜" (13.7 cm) long
13 pieces B – 4¾" (12.1 cm) wide x 10" (25.4 cm) long

From the muslin

Cut 39 strips – 4½" (11.4 cm) x wof

From these 39 strips cut:

12 pieces A – 4½" (11.4 cm) wide x 5⅛" (13 cm) long
76 pieces B – 4½" (11.4 cm) wide x 9¾" (24.8 cm) long
3 pieces C – 4½" (11.4 cm) wide x 14⅜" (36.5 cm) long
3 pieces D – 4½" (11.4 cm) wide x 19" (48.3 cm) long
3 pieces E – 4½" (11.4 cm) wide x 23⅝" (60 cm) long
2 pieces F – 4½" (11.4 cm) wide x 28¼" (71.8 cm) long
2 pieces G – 4½" (11.4 cm) wide x 32⅞" (83.5 cm) long
6 pieces H – 4½" (11.4 cm) wide x 37½" (95.3 cm) long
2 pieces I – 4½" (11.4 cm) wide x 42⅛" (107 cm) long

From Sari Print 1

Cut Backing Panel 1 – 30½" (77.5 cm) wide x 90¼" (229.2 cm) long

From Sari Print 2

Cut Backing Panel 2 – 41¾" (106 cm) wide x 90¼" (229.2 cm) long

From the muslin cut:

Backing Panel 1 – 30¼" (76.8 cm) wide x 90" (228.6 cm) long
Backing Panel 2 – 41½" (105.4 cm) wide x 90" (228.6 cm) long

From the Binding Print

Cut 8 strips – 2½" (6.4 cm) x wof

 Prepare the Sari Fabric Pieces

Note: The sari pieces were cut ¼" (0.6 cm) bigger than the backing muslin in case of slippage during cutting and the fraying nature of the fabric. The ¼" (0.6 cm) seam allowance is included in the muslin pieces. Ensure the sari fabric reaches into the seam allowance when following the steps below.

Tip: Test the spray adhesive on a scrap of each sari fabric to identify if there are any adverse effects.

a. Place one muslin Piece A on a flat surface. Spray with temporary adhesive. Carefully center a Background Sari piece A, **right** side up, on top of the muslin piece, gently pressing to adhere. If there are puckers or air bubbles in the sari fabric, pull it away from the muslin and reposition.

b. Repeat this process to adhere the muslin to all corresponding sari pieces (Quilt Top and Backing). These pieces will be referred to only as the Sari Fabric in the remaining instructions.

 Make the Quilt Top

Note: When sewing the pieces together, match the edges of the muslin and use that edge as the guide for the ¼" (0.6 cm) seam allowance. You will piece the quilt in horizontal rows, beginning with the top row as shown in Figure 1. As you create the rows, stack them carefully or label them so they stay in order.

a. With the **right** sides together, sew the short ends of the sari pieces together into rows, following the guide (see next step). Press seams open.

Horizontal Row 1 – Background Sari piece I; Sari 1 piece B; Sari 2 piece B; Sari 3 piece A

Horizontal Row 2 – Background Sari piece H; Sari 1 piece B; Sari 2 piece B; Sari 3 piece B

Horizontal Row 3 – Background Sari piece G; Sari 1 piece B; Sari 2 piece B; Sari 3 piece B; Sari 1 piece A

Horizontal Row 4 – Background Sari piece F; Sari 1 piece B; Sari 2 piece B; Sari 3 piece B; Sari 1 piece B

Horizontal Row 5 – Background Sari piece E; Sari 1 piece B; Sari 2 piece B; Sari 3 piece B; Sari 1 piece B; Sari 4 piece A

Horizontal Row 6 – Background Sari piece D; Sari 1 piece B; Sari 2 piece B; Sari 3 piece B; Sari 1 piece B; Sari 4 piece B

Horizontal Row 7 – Background Sari piece C; Sari 1 piece B; Sari 2 piece B; Sari 3 piece B; Sari 1 piece B; Sari 4 piece B; Sari 3 piece A

Horizontal Row 8 – Background Sari piece B; Sari 1 piece B; Sari 2 piece B; Sari 3 piece B; Sari 1 piece B; Sari 4 piece B; Sari 3 piece B

Horizontal Row 9 – Background Sari piece A; Sari 1 piece B; Sari 2 piece B; Sari 3 piece B; Sari 1 piece B; Sari 4 piece B; Sari 3 piece B; Background Sari piece A

Horizontal Row 10 – Sari 1 piece B; Sari 2 piece B; Sari 3 piece B; Sari 1 piece B; Sari 4 piece B; Sari 3 piece B; Background Sari piece B

Horizontal Row 11 – Sari 1 piece A; Sari 2 piece B; Sari 3 piece B; Sari 1 piece B; Sari 4 piece B; Sari 3 piece B; Background Sari piece C

Horizontal Row 12 – Sari 2 piece B; Sari 3 piece B; Sari 1 piece B; Sari 4 piece B; Sari 3 piece B; Background Sari piece D

Horizontal Row 13 – Sari 2 piece A; Sari 3 piece B; Sari 1 piece B; Sari 4 piece B; Sari 3 piece B; Background Sari piece E

Horizontal Row 14 – Sari 3 piece B; Sari 1 piece B; Sari 4 piece B; Sari 3 piece B; Background Sari piece F

Horizontal Row 15 – Sari 3 piece A; Sari 1 piece B; Sari 4 piece B; Sari 3 piece B; Background Sari piece G

Horizontal Row 16 – Sari 1 piece B; Sari 4 piece B; Sari 3 piece B; Background Sari piece H

Horizontal Row 17 – Sari 1 piece A; Sari 4 piece B; Sari 3 piece B; Background Sari piece I

Horizontal Row 18 – Sari 4 piece B; Sari 3 piece B; Background Sari piece H; Background Sari piece B

Horizontal Row 19 – Sari 4 piece A; Sari 3 piece B; Background Sari piece H; Background Sari piece C

Horizontal Row 20 – Sari 3 piece B; Background Sari piece H; Background Sari piece D

Horizontal Row 21 – Sari 3 piece A; Background Sari piece H; Background Sari piece E

b. Pin the bottom of Row 1 to the top of Row 2, **right** sides together, and sew. Please note that the vertical seams on each row won't match up. Press the seams in one direction.

c. Repeat Step 3b to connect all 21 rows.

d. Follow the directions in the Glossary and Techniques section (page 168) to square up* the Quilt Top.

Sew the Quilt Back

a. With the **right** sides together, pin together the long edge of one Print 2 Backing Panel with one long edge of the Print 1 Backing Panel. Sew a ½" (1.3 cm) seam. Press the seam open.

b. In the same manner, pin and sew the remaining Print 2 Backing Panel with the opposite long edge of the Print 1 Backing Panel. Press the seam open.

Finish the Quilt

Follow the instructions in the Glossary and Techniques section (page 164) on Assembling the Quilt* and Binding*.

Aspen Branches Quilt

Finished size: 65½" (166.4 cm) wide x 87" (221 cm) long (Twin)

Elegant leaf forms and modern fabrics combine to create a classically beautiful quilt.
Wrap yourself, or someone you love, in the colorful warmth of your own handmade creation!

NOTES

All seams are ¼" (0.6 cm) unless otherwise stated. The seam allowance is included in all measurements. Press all seam allowances to one side as you sew.

DESIGN INFLUENCE

Stripes

TECHNIQUE USED

Patchwork

Figure 1

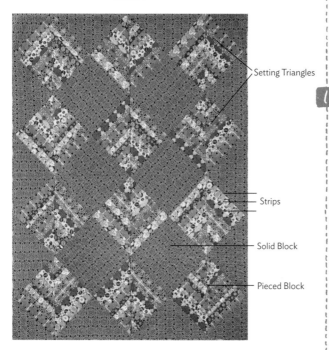

Setting Triangles

Strips

Solid Block

Pieced Block

MATERIALS LIST

Fabrics

Use Figure 1 as a guide
From 44" (112 cm) wide light- to mid-weight fabric

½ yard (0.46 m) each of 9 coordinating prints for the Strips in the pieced blocks

3 yards (2.74 m) of coordinating solid or print for the Solid Blocks and Setting Triangles

⅝ yard (0.57 m) of coordinating solid or print for the Binding

5¼ yards (4.8 m) of coordinating solid or print for the Backing

OTHER SUPPLIES

72" x 93" (182.9 x 236.2 cm) piece of extra-loft batting (Fairfield)
2 large spools of coordinating all-purpose thread (Coats)

ADDITIONAL TOOLS NEEDED

Masking tape and marker
Square 16½" (41.9 cm) ruler or larger quilter's ruler
1 package of large safety pins
1 standard hand-sewing needle

Cut Out the Fabric Strips

Label the fabric prints 1 through 9 as a guide, using masking tape and a marker.
Use your rotary cutter, mat, and ruler to cut the Strips listed below.

From Fabric 1
Cut 2 strips – 3" (7.6 cm) x width of fabric* (wof)
Cut 2 strips – 2¼" (5.7 cm) x wof
Cut 1 strip – 1¾" (4.4 cm) x wof
Cut 2 strips – 1½" (3.8 cm) x wof

From Fabric 2
Cut 2 strips – 2¼" (5.7 cm) x wof
Cut 2 strips – 2" (5.1 cm) x wof
Cut 2 strips – 1¾" (4.4 cm) x wof

From Fabric 3
Cut 2 strips – 3" (7.6 cm) x wof
Cut 1 strip – 2" (5.1 cm) x wof
Cut 2 strips – 1¾" (4.4 cm) x wof
Cut 2 strips – 1½" (3.8 cm) x wof

From Fabric 4

Cut 2 strips – 3" (7.6 cm) x wof
Cut 2 strips – 2¼" (5.7 cm) x wof
Cut 2 strips – 2" (5.1 cm) x wof
Cut 1 strip – 1½" (3.8 cm) x wof

From Fabric 5

Cut 1 strip – 2¼" (5.7 cm) x wof
Cut 1 strip – 2" (5.1 cm) x wof
Cut 2 strips – 1¾" (4.4 cm) x wof
Cut 2 strips – 1½" (3.8 cm) x wof

From Fabric 6

Cut 2 strips – 3" (7.6 cm) x wof
Cut 1 strip – 2" (5.1 cm) x wof
Cut 2 strips – 2¼" (5.7 cm) x wof
Cut 1 strip – 1¾" (4.4 cm) x wof
Cut 1 strip – 1½" (3.8 cm) x wof

From Fabric 7

Cut 2 strips – 3" (7.6 cm) x wof
Cut 1 strip – 2¼" (5.7 cm) x wof
Cut 1 strip – 2" (5.1 cm) x wof
Cut 2 strips – 1¾" (4.4 cm) x wof
Cut 1 strip – 1½" (3.8 cm) x wof

From Fabric 8

Cut 2 strips – 3 " (7.6 cm) x wof
Cut 1 strip – 2¼" (5.7 cm) x wof
Cut 2 strips – 2" (5.1 cm) x wof
Cut 1 strip – 1¾" (4.4 cm) x wof
Cut 1 strip – 1½" (3.8 cm) x wof

From Fabric 9

Cut 1 strip – 2¼" (5.7 cm) x wof
Cut 2 strips – 2" (5.1 cm) x wof
Cut 1 strip – 1¾" (4.4 cm) x wof
Cut 2 strips – 1½" (3.8 cm) x wof

From the fabric for the Solid Blocks and Setting Triangles:

The Setting Triangles and Corner Triangles fill in the gaps around the edges of the quilt when the blocks on are placed on point like diamonds. They are cut oversized to allow for a small border between the Binding and the points of the pieced Blocks.

Cut 6 – 15½" (39.3 cm) squares for Solid Blocks
Cut 3 – 24¾" (62.9 cm) squares for the six Setting Triangles
Cut 2 – 13" (33 cm) squares for the four Corner Triangles

From the 24¾" (62.9 cm) squares, cut 12 triangles as follows:

On the **right** side of the first square, line up the edge of your ruler with the points on the top left and bottom right corners, then, using your ruler and chalk pencil, draw a diagonal line between them.

Draw a second diagonal line connecting opposite corners on the same square. Using your scissors, cut along each marked line. Repeat these steps on the remaining two 24¾" (62.9 cm) squares.

Note: You will use only 10 of these 12 squares.

Cut the two 13" (33 cm) squares in half as follows:

Mark one diagonal on each of these blocks and cut. Please set these four triangles aside for now.

From the Binding fabric:

Cut 8 strips – 2½" (6.4 cm) x wof

From the Backing fabric:

Cut 1 Center Back Panel – 37" (94 cm) wide x 93" (236.2 cm) long
Cut 2 Side Back Panels – 18" (45.7 cm) wide x 93" (236.2 cm) long

 Attach the Strips to Make the Pieced Fabric

Note: A Strip Set is a set of Strips stitched together in the order indicated to make a pieced fabric length.

a. On a large, flat surface, lay out the Strips for Strip Set A following the order in Table 1. Place them from left to right with the **right** side facing up.

TABLE 1
FABRIC ASSIGNMENT AND CUT WIDTH FOR EACH STRIP SET

	3" (7.6 cm)	2" (5.1 cm)	1½" (3.8 cm)	2¼" (5.7 cm)	1¾" (4.4 cm)	2" (5.1 cm)	1½" (3.8 cm)	2¼" (5.7 cm)	1¾" (4.4 cm)	3" (7.6 cm)
Strip Set A	Fab 1	Fab 2	Fab 3	Fab 4	Fab 5	Fab 6	Fab 7	Fab 8	Fab 9	Fab 1
Strip Set B	Fab 3	Fab 4	Fab 5	Fab 6	Fab 7	Fab 8	Fab 9	Fab 1	Fab 2	Fab 3
Strip Set C	Fab 4	Fab 5	Fab 6	Fab 7	Fab 8	Fab 9	Fab 1	Fab 2	Fab 3	Fab 4
Strip Set D	Fab 6	Fab 7	Fab 8	Fab 9	Fab 1	Fab 2	Fab 3	Fab 4	Fab 5	Fab 6
Strip Set E	Fab 7	Fab 8	Fab 9	Fab 1	Fab 2	Fab 3	Fab 4	Fab 5	Fab 6	Fab 7
Strip Set F	Fab 8	Fab 9	Fab 1	Fab 2	Fab 3	Fab 4	Fab 5	Fab 6	Fab 7	Fab 8

Tip: When stitching Strips together, start sewing at alternate ends to avoid the Strips getting distorted and curving like a rainbow.

b. Starting with Strip Set A, place the first two pieces **right** sides together, matching one long edge, and pin them in place. Stitch along the pinned edges. Press seam allowance to one side.

c. Place the third Strip along the other long edge of the second strip, **right** sides together, and pin it in place. Stitch along the pinned edge; press.

d. Continue attaching Strips in this manner until you have all ten Strips attached. The finished pieced fabric should measure 16½" (42 cm) x wof. Mark this as piece A.

e. Referring to Table 1, repeat Steps 2a to 2d to create Strip Sets B through F. (See Figure 2.)

Figure 2

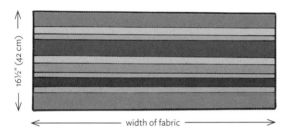

16½" (42 cm)

← width of fabric →

Make the Pieced Blocks

In this step you will use a shortcut technique to create two blocks at once. Once you see how it works, you'll want to use it in other quilting projects.

a. On a flat surface, place Strip Set A with **right** side facing up. Cut two 16½" (42 cm) squares, and label each square with masking tape and pen. Set them aside.

b. Repeat this with each of the five remaining pieced fabric lengths (Strip Sets B through F).

c. Select two squares, one from Strip Set A and one from Strip Set C. Press the seam allowances on the square from Strip Set C so they are facing the opposite direction to those on the square from Strip Set A.

d. On a flat surface, place the two squares with **right** sides together, matching the seams on the two, and pin them in place. (See Figure 3.) Note: Seam allowances on the **wrong** side of the squares are not shown in Figures 3, 4, and 5.

Figure 3

Two 16½" (42 cm) squares from different Strip Sets, **right** sides together. (Strip seam allowances not shown.)

e. On the **wrong** side of the top square, use a ruler and chalk pencil to draw a line diagonally across the square from the top left corner to the bottom right. Line up the seams on each side close to the drawn line and pin them in place. (See Figure 4.)

Figure 4

Draw a diagonal line on the **wrong** side of the top square. (Strip seam allowances not shown.)

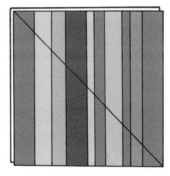

f. Stitch ¼" (0.6 cm) to the right of the diagonal line. Rotate the squares and sew ¼" (0.6 cm) from the other side of the drawn line. (See Figure 5.)

Figure 5

Stitch ¼" (0.6 cm) from each side of the diagonal line, then cut along the line. (Strip seam allowances not shown.)

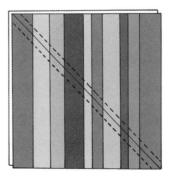

g. Use your scissors to cut along the drawn line, making two Pieced Blocks. Unfold the blocks and press the seam allowances to one side.

h. Repeat Steps 3d to 3g using the remaining ten pieced squares, placing them together as shown in Table 2. This will make ten additional Pieced Blocks.

TABLE 2 PIECED SQUARE PAIRS

A	B	B	C	D
E	D	F	E	F

4 Square Up* Each Quilt Block

a. Lay the first Block **right** side up. Using your rotary cutter and square ruler, trim the Block down to a 15½" (39.4 cm) square, making sure the diagonal line on the ruler matches the diagonal seam on the Block and intersects at the corners.

b. Repeat Step 4a for the remaining eleven Pieced Blocks.

5 Attach the Blocks in Rows

The Quilt Center is pieced together in diagonal rows. The Corner Triangles will be attached later. Following Figure 6, lay out the Pieced Blocks, Solid Blocks, and Setting Triangles to decide on placement. Make sure to alternate the direction of the Pieced Blocks, row by row, keeping the center seams vertical throughout the Quilt.

Note: Always press the seam allowances toward the Solid Blocks or Setting Triangles in Steps 5a to 5d as you sew.

a. Starting at the top right corner for Row 1, place the first Pieced Block and the first Setting Triangle with **right** sides together, matching the edges. Pin them in place. Stitch along the pinned edge. Note: The side points of the Setting Triangles will hang over the Pieced Blocks. It is important to follow Figure 6 to make sure the Setting Triangles are attached facing the correct direction.

b. Repeat Step 5a to attach the other Setting Triangle in this row. Set this diagonal row down to start your layout.

c. For the next row, place the next Pieced Block and Setting Triangle with **right** sides together, matching the edges and referring to the diagram for the orientation of the Pieced Block. Pin them in place and stitch. Add a Solid Block to the opposite side. Continue to attach the remaining Blocks in this row, ending with a Setting Triangle. Set this diagonal row into your layout.

d. Repeat Step 5c to to complete the remaining diagonal rows, continuing to follow Figure 6.

Figure 6

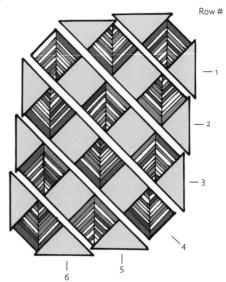

Sew the Pieced Blocks and Solid Blocks together in each row.

6 Attach the Rows and Corner Triangles

a. Starting at the top right corner, place the first and second diagonal rows **right** sides together, matching the seams of the Pieced and Solid Blocks, and pin them in place. Stitch along the pinned edge and press the seams in one direction.

b. With **right** sides together, match the opposite edge of the second row with the third row and pin it in place. Stitch along the pinned edge and press the seams in the same direction.

c. Repeat Steps 6a and 6b to sew the three remaining rows in place.

d. Next, fold the first Corner Triangle in half across the long diagonal edge and finger press* to mark the center of the long edge.

e. Then fold the top left edge of the first Pieced Block in half and press a crease along the folded edge to mark the center of the Block.

f. Place the Corner Triangle on top of the Pieced Block, **right** sides together, matching the center crease lines, and pin in place. Stitch along the pinned edge.

7 Make the Quilt Back

a. Fold the first Back Panel in half across the width, matching the short ends. Press a crease at both ends of the folded edge to mark the center of the panel. Then fold it in half again and press to mark the quarter points. Repeat this step to mark the center and quarter points on the other two Back Panels.

b. Place one of the Side Back Panels and the Center Back Panel **right** sides together, matching one long edge at the half and quarter points. Pin in place. Stitch a ½" (1.3 cm) seam along the pinned edge. Press the seam allowances open.

c. Repeat Step 7b to attach the second Side Back Panel to the other long edge of the Center Back second Panel.

8 Finish the Quilt

Follow the instructions in the Glossary and Techniques section (page 164) on Assembling the Quilt* and Binding*, skipping the instructions for sewing the Back Panels.

Whimsy Quilt

Finished size: 89¾" (228 cm) wide x 96¼" (24.5 cm) long (Queen)

Happiness is personified in this warm and colorful quilt.
Bold vintage prints and Log Cabin rhythms dance together as perfect partners!

NOTES

All seams are ¼" (0.6 cm) unless otherwise stated. The seam allowance is included in all measurements. Press all seam allowances to one side as you sew.

DESIGN INFLUENCE

Wonky Log Cabin

TECHNIQUE USED

Patchwork

Figure 1

Main Panel Separating Strip

Left Main Panel

Right Main Panel

1
2
3
4

Block 1   Block 2   Block 3   Block 4

Stripes

MATERIALS LIST

Fabrics

Use Figure 1 as a guide

From 44" (112 cm) wide light- to mid-weight fabric

1½ yards (1.37 m) of one print for Left Main Panel

2⅛ yards (1.94 m) of second print for Right Main Panel

⅛ yard (0.11 m) of print or solid for Main Panel Separating Strip

⅜ yard (0.34 m) of print or solid for Bottom Stripe 1

⅜ yard (0.34 m) of print or solid for Bottom Stripe 2

⅜ yard (0.34 m) of print or solid for Bottom Stripe 3

⅝ yard (0.57 m) of print or solid for Bottom Stripe 4

5 to 5¼ yards (4.57 to 4.8 m) total of fabric scraps for Log Cabin Blocks (we used 16 different fabrics, mixing prints, solids, and other fabrics used within the quilt)

7¾ yards (7.1 m) fabric print or solid for Backing

¾ yard (0.7 m) fabric print or solid for Binding

OTHER SUPPLIES

110" (279.4 cm) square piece of low-loft batting (Fairfield)

2 large spools of coordinating all-purpose thread (Coats)

ADDITIONAL TOOLS

Masking tape and marker

Safety pins (large size)

1 standard hand-sewing needle

Cut Out the Fabric Pieces

Use your rotary cutter, mat, and ruler to cut the specific amounts listed.

Note: When cutting the Block pieces, use the masking tape and marker to label them, then sort them into piles based on the block number: 1, 2, 3, or 4.

Left Main Panel Fabric

Cut 1 panel – 42½" x 51¾" (108 x 131.4 cm)

Right Main Panel Fabric

Cut 1 panel – 36" x 51¾" (91.4 x 131.4 cm)

Cut 1 panel – 42" x 11¼" (106.4 x 28.6 cm)
Cut 1 panel – 10¼" x 11¼" (26 x 28.6 cm)

Main Panel Separator Strips
Cut 2 strips – 1½" (3.8 cm) x width of fabric* (wof)

Bottom Stripe 1
Cut 3 strips – 3½" (3.8 cm) x wof

Bottom Stripe 2
Cut 3 strips – 3½" (3.8 cm) x wof

Bottom Stripe 3
Cut 3 strips – 3½" (3.8 cm) x wof

Bottom Stripe 4 Fabric
Cut 3 strips – 6½" (16.5 cm) x wof

Patchwork Block Scrap Fabric
For Block 1 – use random fabrics, cut to these sizes:
Cut piece 1A – 1½" x 5¼" (3.8 x 13.3 cm)
Cut piece 1B – 5½" x 5¼" (14 x 13.3 cm)
Cut piece 1C – 3" x 5¼" (7.6 x 13.3 cm)
Cut piece 1D – 2¾" x 9" (7 x 22.9 cm)
Cut piece 1E – 2½" x 7½" (6.4 x 19.1 cm)
Cut piece 1F – 5½" x 7½" (14 x 19.1 cm)
Cut piece 1G – 1¼" x 16" (3.2 x 40.6 cm)
Cut piece 1H – 2" x 8¼" (5.1 x 21 cm)
Cut piece 1I – 2" x 2¼" (5.1 x 5.7 cm)
Cut piece 1J – 2¼" x 16" (5.7 x 40.6 cm)
Cut piece 1K – 1¾" x 10" (4.4 x 25.4 cm)
Cut piece 1L – 2¾" x 18¾" (7 x 47.6 cm)
Cut piece 1M – 2¾" x 18¾" (7 x 47.6 cm)
Cut piece 1N – 1½" x 18¾" (3.8 x 47.6 cm)
Cut piece 1O – 3" x 15½" (7.6 x 39.4 cm)
Cut piece 1P – 2½" x 21¼" (6.4 x 54 cm)
Cut piece 1Q – 3½" x 17½" (8.9 x 44.5 cm)
Cut piece 1R – 2½" x 24¼" (6.4 x 61.6 cm)
Cut piece 1S – 2¾" x 19½" (7 x 49.5 cm)
Cut piece 1T – 3½" x 26½" (8.9 x 67.3 cm)
Cut piece 1U – 4½" x 22½" (11.4 x 57.2 cm)

For Block 2 – use random fabrics, cut to these sizes:
Cut piece 2A – 3" x 3¼" (7.6 x 8.3 cm)
Cut piece 2B – 3½" x 3¼" (8.9 x 8.3 cm)
Cut piece 2C – 1½" x 3¼" (3.8 x 8.3 cm)
Cut piece 2D – 2⅜" x 7" (6 x 17.8 cm)
Cut piece 2E – 3" x 5⅛" (7.6 x 13 cm)
Cut piece 2F – 2⅜" x 9½" (6 x 24.1 cm)
Cut piece 2G – 4¼" x 9½" (10.8 x 24.1 cm)
Cut piece 2H – 5¾" x 10¾" (13.3 x 27.3 cm)
Cut piece 2I – 3½" x 10¾" (8.9 x 27.3 cm)
Cut piece 2J – 3" x 17¾" (7.6 x 45.1 cm)
Cut piece 2K – 4" x 13¼" (10.2 x 33.7 cm)
Cut piece 2L – 3" x 17¾" (7.6 x 45.1 cm)
Cut piece 2M – 3" x 4" (7.6 x 10.2 cm)
Cut piece 2N – 1¾" x 21¼" (4.4 x 54 cm)
Cut piece 2O – 3" x 17" (7.6 x 43.2 cm)
Cut piece 2P – 2" x 17" (5.1 x 43.2 cm)
Cut piece 2Q – 2¾" x 25¼" (7 x 64.1 cm)
Cut piece 2R – 2¾" x 19¼" (7 x 48.9 cm)
Cut piece 2S – 2¾" x 27½" (7 x 69.9 cm)
Cut piece 2T – 3½" x 21½" (8.9 x 54.6 cm)
Cut piece 2U – 2" x 30½" (5.1 x 77.5 cm)

For Block 3 – use random fabrics, cut to these sizes:
Cut piece 3A – 5½" x 4½" (14 x 11.4 cm)
Cut piece 3B – 3½" x 4½" (8.9 x 11.4 cm)
Cut piece 3C – 2½" x 4½" (6.4 x 11.4 cm)
Cut piece 3D – 2" x 4½" (5.1 x 11.4 cm)
Cut piece 3E – 2¼" x 12" (5.7 x 30.5 cm)
Cut piece 3F – 1¼" x 12" (3.2 x 30.5 cm)
Cut piece 3G – 1¾" x 12" (4.4 x 30.5 cm)
Cut piece 3H – 2½" x 8¼" (6.4 x 21 cm)
Cut piece 3I – 1¾" x 14" (4.4 x 35.6 cm)
Cut piece 3J – 1¾" x 9½" (4.4 x 24.1 cm)
Cut piece 3K – 1¼" x 9½" (3.2 x 24.1 cm)
Cut piece 3L – 1¼" x 9½" (3.2 x 24.1 cm)
Cut piece 3M – 3" x 16¾" (7.6 x 42.5 cm)
Cut piece 3N – 2" x 16¾" (5.1 x 42.5 cm)
Cut piece 3O – 2½" x 16¾" (6.4 x 42.5 cm)
Cut piece 3P – 2¼" x 15½" (5.7 x 39.4 cm)
Cut piece 3Q – 2⅝" x 15½" (6.7 x 39.4 cm)
Cut piece 3R – 1⅝" x 15½" (4.1 x 39.4 cm)
Cut piece 3S – 1¾" x 21¾" (4.4 x 55.2 cm)
Cut piece 3T – 2¾" x 21¾" (7 x 55.2 cm)
Cut piece 3U – 2" x 21¾" (5.1 x 55.2 cm)
Cut piece 3V – 1¾" x 20½" (4.4 x 52.1 cm)
Cut piece 3W – 2" x 23" (5.1 x 58.4 cm)
Cut piece 3X – 2" x 23" (5.1 x 58.4 cm)
Cut piece 3Y – 8" x 23½" (20.3 x 59.7 cm)

For Block 4 – use random fabrics, cut to these sizes:
Cut piece 4A – 2" x 5¼" (5 x 13.3 cm)
Cut piece 4B – 2½" x 5¼" (6.4 x 13.3 cm)
Cut piece 4C – 1¼" x 5¼" (3.2 x 13.3 cm)

Cut piece 4D – 7½" x 5¼" (19.1 x 13.3 cm)
Cut piece 4E – 2" x 5¼" (5.1 x 13.3 cm)
Cut piece 4F – 2½" x 5¼" (6.4 x 13.3 cm)
Cut piece 4G – 3¼" x 15¼" (8.3 x 38.7 cm)
Cut piece 4H – 2" x 8" (5.1 x 20.3 cm)
Cut piece 4I – 2¾" x 13¼" (7 x 33.7 cm)
Cut piece 4J – 2¾" x 4" (7 cm x 10.2 cm)
Cut piece 4K – 2¾" x 16¾" (7 x 42.5 cm)
Cut piece 4L – 2½" x 12½" (6.4 x 31.8 cm)
Cut piece 4M – 2¼" x 18¾" (5.7 x 47.6 cm)
Cut piece 4N – 2½" x 14¼" (6.4 x 36.2 cm)
Cut piece 4O – 2½" x 20¾" (6.4 x 52.7 cm)
Cut piece 4P – 2¼" x 16¼" (5.7 x 41.3 cm)
Cut piece 4Q – 1½" x 22½" (3.8 x 57.2 cm)
Cut piece 4R – 2¾" x 22½" (7 x 57.2 cm)
Cut piece 4S – 3½" x 19½" (8.9 x 49.5 cm)
Cut piece 4T – 3¾" x 25½" (9.5 x 64.8 cm)
Cut piece 4U – 2½" x 22¾" (6.4 x 57.8 cm)
Cut piece 4V – 3½" x 22¾" (8.9 x 57.8 cm)

Backing Fabric
Cut 3 panels – 93" (236.2 cm) long x wof

Binding Fabric
Cut 10 strips – 2½" (6.4 cm) x wof

Make the Main Panel
a. Piece together the Right Main Panel pieces. Pin the 42" x 11¼" (106.7 x 28.6 cm) panel and the 10¼" x 11¼" (26 x 28.6 cm) panel **right** sides together along the 11¼" (28.6 cm) edges. Stitch this pinned edge. Then, match the long edge of this sewn panel to the long edge of the 36" x 51¾" (91.4 x 131.4 cm) panel, matching **right** sides together, and pin in place. Stitch along this pinned edge.
b. Cut the selvages* off the two Main Panel Separating Strips and pin them **right** sides together, matching two short ends. Stitch along the pinned edges. Trim the strip to 51¾" (131.4 cm) long.
c. Now pin and sew the Left Main Panel and the pieced Right Main Panel to either side of the Separator Strip, **right** sides together. Press the seam allowances toward the Separator Strip.

Make Block 1
(Finished size 22" [55.9 cm] wide x 30" [76.2 cm] long)
Use the Block 1 diagram (Figure 2) as a placement guide when sewing the pieces together.

a. Start by pinning 1A to 1B **right** sides together along two 5¼" (13.3 cm) sides. Stitch along the pinned edges.
b. Then pin 1B to 1C **right** sides together along two matching sides. Stitch along the pinned edges.
c. Continue to pin, sew, and press pieces 1D through 1U together, working in alphabetical order, following the diagram. Note: Pieces 1I to 1J will be sewn together before attaching to the Block.

Figure 2

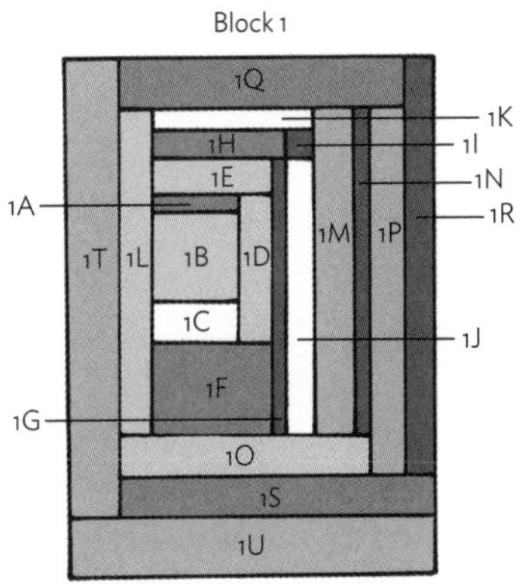

Block 1

Make Block 2
(Finished size 22½" [57.2 cm] wide x 30" [76.2 cm] long)
Use the Block 2 diagram (Figure 3) as a placement guide when sewing two pieces together.

a. Start by pinning 2A to 2B **right** sides together along the 3¼" (8.2 cm) sides. Stitch along the pinned edges.
b. Then pin 2B to 2C **right** sides together along two matching sides. Stitch along the pinned edges.
c. Continue to pin, sew, and press pieces 2D to 2U together, working in alphabetical order, following the diagram. Note: Pieces 2L to 2M will be sewn together before attaching to the Block.

Figure 3

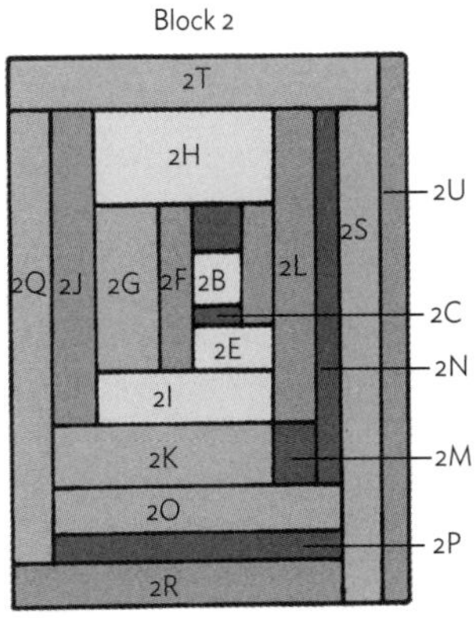

Block 2

Make Block 3

(Finished size 23" [58.4 cm] wide x 30" [76.2 cm] long)

Use the Block 3 diagram (Figure 4) as a placement guide when sewing the pieces together

a. Start by pinning 3A to 3B **right** sides together along two 4½" (11.4 cm) sides. Stitch along the pinned edges.

b. Then pin 3B to 3C **right** sides together along two matching sides. Stitch along the pinned edges.

c. Continue to pin, sew, and press pieces 3D to 3Y together, working in alphabetical order, following the diagram.

Figure 4

Block 3

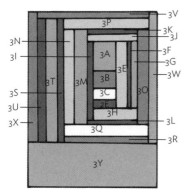

Make Block 4

(Finished size 22¼" [56.5 cm] wide x 30" [76.2 cm] long)

Use the Block 4 diagram (Figure 5) as a placement guide when sewing two pieces together.

a. Start by pinning 4A to 4B **right** sides together along two 5¼" (13.3 cm) sides. Stitch along the pinned edges.

b. Then pin 4B to 4C **right** sides together along two matching sides. Stitch along the pinned edges.

c. Continue to pin, sew, and press pieces 4D to 4V together, working in alphabetical order, following the diagram. Note: Pieces 4I to 4J will be sewn together before attaching to the Block.

Figure 5

Block 4

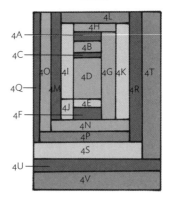

Make the Bottom Stripes Panel

a. Start by cutting the selvages from the Bottom Stripe 1 fabric strips.

b. Then pin the three strips **right** sides together along the short ends. Sew along the pinned edges to make one long strip. Trim this strip to 90¼" (229.2 cm) long.

c. Repeat steps 7a and 7b to make the Bottom Stripes 2, 3, and 4.

d. Sew the Bottom Stripes together by matching the stripes along the long edges in order: 1, 2, 3, and 4. Tip: When stitching the Bottom Stripes together, start sewing at alternate ends to avoid the stripes getting distorted and curving like a rainbow.

Make the Quilt Top

Use Figure 1 as a guide.

a. Sew the four blocks together along the long edges in order: 1, 2, 3, and 4.

b. Sew the Block Panel to the bottom of the Main Panel.

c. Sew the Stripe Panel to the bottom of the Block Panel.

Finish the Quilt

Follow the instructions in the Glossary and Techniques section (page 164) on Assembling the Quilt* and Binding*.

Trappings and Treasures

Accessories and Small Gifts

Create statement pieces with these beautifully embellished projects. Whether you are updating your style or gifting a treasure, patchwork has never been prettier!

Statement Necklace

Finished dimensions: Patchwork Pendant: 3¼" (8.3 cm) wide x 4⅝" (11.8 cm) tall

Length of ribbons: 18" (45.7 cm) long • Bead Fob: 3" (7.6 cm)

The prettiest of stitches for your personal adornment!
Add your delicate beading and handwork and make this an heirloom to treasure forever.

NOTES

All seams are ¼" (0.6 cm) unless otherwise stated. The seam allowance is included in all measurements.

DESIGN INFLUENCE

Improv Log Cabin

TECHNIQUES USED

Patchwork

Beadwork

Tassel Making

Figure 1

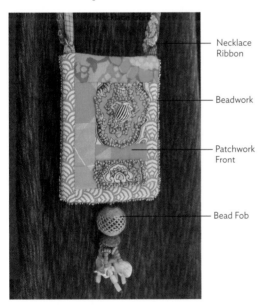

MATERIALS LIST

Fabrics

Use Figure 1 as a guide

An assortment of fabric scraps and ribbons in varying widths for the patchwork on the Necklace Front

6" (15.2 cm) square piece of muslin

6" (15.2 cm) square piece of fabric for the Back

A piece of silk or voile fabric, at least 31" x 6" (78.7 x 15.2 cm)
(I used a piece of antique silk sari fabric) for Necklace Ribbons

OTHER SUPPLIES

A 6" (15.2 cm) square piece of Hi-Loft Quilt Batting (Fairfield)

Several different beads with ¼" (0.6 cm) diameter center holes for embellishing the Necklace Ribbons

An assortment of seed beads, small beads, buttons, or pins for embellishing the Necklace Front and edges

1 spool of coordinating or neutral all-purpose sewing thread (Coats)

1 spool of transparent thread (Coats)

ADDITONAL TOOLS NEEDED

Large safety pins

Walking foot for your sewing machine (optional)

Tube turner (Quick Turn Tube Turner by Prym-Dritz)

Turning tool (Prym-Dritz)

1 standard hand-sewing needle

1 beading needle (Prym-Dritz)

Needle-nose pliers

MATERIALS FOR OPTIONAL BEAD FOB

1½ yards (1.37 m) of 1 mm cotton braiding cord (Natural Cotton Braiding Cord by Clubhouse Crafts)

1 or 2 main beads ⅝" to ¾" (1.6 to 1.9 cm) in diameter
Note: Make sure the center hole is large enough for 4 strands of the cotton braiding cord to pass through

30 to 32 assorted beads ¼" to ½" (0.6 to 1.3 cm) in diameter Note: Make sure the center holes of the beads are large enough for one strand of cotton braiding cord to pass through

Fabric glue (Aleene's Jewel-It Washable Glue)

Make the Necklace Front

a. Start by selecting a print you'd like to use as your center block. This will be the focal element of your Necklace Front. Then choose several coordinating fabrics and/or ribbons for your remaining strips. Play with the arrangement of

your pieces to create your own individual design, using the improvisational patchwork technique from Chapter 1, keeping in mind a finished size. The finished dimensions for my necklace are 3¼" (8.3 cm) wide x 4⅝" (11.8 cm) tall. Scale yours to your liking. Once you find an arrangement you are happy with, take a picture for easy reference.

b. Following your layout, sew the center block and one of the strips together using a ¼" (0.6 cm) seam allowance and pressing the seams in one direction. Continue sewing strips around the center block until the Necklace Front measures 1" (2.5 cm) larger on each side than your planned finished size.

c. Now, using the Necklace Front as a template, cut one piece from the batting and one from the muslin. Layer these pieces together, sandwiching the batting in between the Front and the muslin. Safety-pin the layers together.

d. If you have a walking foot for your sewing machine, put it on now. With transparent thread in your needle and all-purpose thread in the bobbin, machine quilt through all the layers by stitching-in-the-ditch* along all the seams, working from the center of the piece out. Switch to your standard sewing machine foot.

e. Next, use a rotary cutter, mat, and ruler to square up* the Front piece, leaving a ⅜" (1 cm) seam allowance on each side.

f. Cut one Necklace Back using the Front as a pattern piece and set aside.

Make and Attach the Necklace Ribbons

a. Using a rotary cutter, mat, and ruler, cut the silk or voile fabric into four strips, each measuring 1½" (3.8 cm) wide x 31" (78.7 cm) long.

b. Fold each strip **right** sides together, matching the long edges, and sew them together using a ⅜" (1 cm) seam. Use the tube turner to gently turn the fabric ribbons **right** side out; press flat.

c. Now, stack two Necklace Ribbons on top of each other and pin the ends to the **right** side of the Necklace Front just inside the ⅜" (1 cm) seam allowance on one side, matching the ribbon ends with the top edge. Position the other two ribbon ends on the other side of the Necklace Front in the same manner. Use a machine basting* stitch and sew across the top edge of the Front to hold the ribbon ends in place. These will get sewn in permanently in Step 3.

Sew the Necklace Front and Back Together

a. Pin the Necklace Front and Back, **right** sides together, matching all the edges. Tuck loose ends of the ribbons in between the two layers to keep them from getting caught in the stitching. Sew around all the sides, using a ⅜" (1 cm) seam allowance, pivoting* at all the corners and leaving a 2" (5.1 cm) opening for turning along the bottom edge. Trim* all the corners, making sure not to clip your stitching.

b. Turn the necklace **right** side out, gently pushing out the corners with a turning tool*. Press flat. Slipstitch* the opening closed if you are not adding a Beaded Fob.

4 Embellish the Necklace

Note: The embellishments are necessary to give the Necklace some weight to allow it to lie properly.

a. Decorate your one-of-a-kind Necklace Ribbons by threading them through large-eyed beads and tying knots around the beads in random places. Try your necklace on as you are working to check the length, making any adjustments as necessary. Tie a final knot in your ribbons at your desired length, trimming any excess length.

b. Thread the beading needle with a double strand of transparent thread and knot the ends. Tip: Kink the thread with a pair of needle-nose pliers where you want the knot to go. When you tie the knot at this kink, it will be less likely to shift. Use the pliers to help pull the knot tight. Pull the needle up through the bottom seam and out through the Necklace Front in the place where you wish to start your beadwork. Pull the knot gently so that it is pulled into the seam and hidden. Take a few stitches through the fabric to secure your starting point, ending with the needle on the **right** side of the Front.

c. To embellish your Necklace Front, decide which areas of the Front you wish to bead. Work with only one to three beads at a time to keep them from being too loose when you stitch them to the Necklace Front. String selected beads onto your needle, pushing the beads down to where the thread comes through the fabric. Push the needle back into the fabric through the hole where the base of the thread is. Make sure to pull tight enough on the threads that the beads are touching the fabric. Pull any loose threads taut.

d. Now come back up through the layers next to where you ended stitching the previous set of beads and pass the needle back through the last bead in the set. Then thread the needle again with one to three beads, pushing them down to the base of the thread and against the previous beads. Push the needle back through where the base of the thread is. Continue using this method to bead around the Necklace Front. When you finish, take a few stitches in one place and tie a knot. Push the needle back through the Front below the knot to the Necklace Back and gently pull the knot to the inside of the necklace. Clip the thread tail close to the Back.

e. Use the same method in Steps 4b to 4d to bead the outside edge of your necklace, hiding the thread knots inside the seams.

5 Make the Bead Fob for the Bottom of the Necklace

a. If you'd like to add a fob, measure and cut the cotton cord into four equal lengths.

b. Tie a knot at one end of each length of cording. If desired, apply a small dab of fabric glue to secure the knot. Let the glue dry before continuing.

c. Now thread seven or eight beads onto each length of cording in an order that is pleasing to you. Tip: Before threading your beads, dab a bit of fabric glue on the end of your cord and let dry. This will keep the cording from fraying on the end.

d. Bring the unknotted ends of all four cords together and tie them together in a secure knot right above the beading you just did in Step 5c.

e. Now, add one of the large main beads by threading all four cords through the bead hole. Tie another knot at the top of the bead to secure. Add a second bead and knot if desired.

f. Slip the unknotted cording ends up into the opening at the bottom of the necklace. Thread a hand-sewing needle with a double strand of thread and stitch the cords to the inside of the Necklace Front to secure. Slipstitch the opening in the necklace closed.

Tapestry Shoulder Bag

Finished size: 18" (42.5 cm) wide x 13" (33 cm) tall (excluding straps)

Easy piecing highlights your favorite fabric combinations in this fashionable daytime run-around bag.

NOTES

All seams are ½" (1.3 cm) unless otherwise stated. The seam allowance is included in all pattern pieces.

DESIGN INFLUENCE

Log Cabin

TECHNIQUE USED

Patchwork

MATERIALS LIST

Fabrics

From 44" (112 cm) wide light- to mid-weight cotton quilting fabric

⅝ yard (0.57 m) of print for Center Square and Patchwork

¼ yard (0.23 m) each of 4 coordinating prints for Patchwork

⅝ yard (0.57 m) of coordinating print for Cording Covering and Strap

1¼ yards (1.14 m) of coordinating print for Lining and Cell Phone Pocket

⅞ yard (0.80 m) of muslin for the backing of the patchwork panels

OTHER SUPPLIES

3¼ yards (3 m) of 20" (51 cm) wide fusible woven interfacing (Pellon SF101)

3⅜ yards (3.1 m) of cotton filler cord size ¹²⁄₃₂" (1 cm) (Wrights)

1 spool of coordinating all-purpose thread (Coats)

1 spool of button and carpet thread (Coats)

ADDITIONAL TOOLS NEEDED

Zipper foot

Turning tool (Dritz)

1 standard hand-sewing needle

1 sheet of dressmaker's tracing paper (Dritz)

Transparent tape

1 large-eye hand-sewing needle (Dritz)

1 large safety pin

 Cut Out the Pattern Pieces

From the pattern sheet included with this book, cut out Main Panel

 Cut Out the Fabric Pieces

Center Square and Patchwork Fabric

Using your rotary cutter, mat, and ruler:

Cut 2 strips 2¼" (5.7 cm) x width of fabric* (wof)

Cut 2 strips 1¾" (4.4 cm) x wof

Open the remaining fabric **right** side facing up. Use your ruler and marking pen to measure and mark an 8½" (21.6 cm) square on-point (diagonally like a diamond shape) directly onto the fabric, centering the square over the part of the fabric design you wish to feature.

Cut 1 square

Repeat measuring and cutting a second square on another part of the fabric.

Coordinating Patchwork Fabrics

Using your rotary cutter, mat, and ruler:

Cut 2 strips each 2¼" (5.7 cm) x wof

Cut 2 strips each 1¾" (4.4 cm) x wof

Cording Fabric

Fold the fabric on the bias*. Follow the instructions in the Glossary and Techniques section (page 164) for marking and cutting fabric on the bias.

Cut enough 2⅛" (5.4 cm) wide bias strips to make one strip 37" (94 cm) long for the bottom of the bag

Cut enough 3½" (8.9 cm) wide bias strips to make two strips, each 38" (96.5 cm) long, for the strap covers

Muslin

Cut 2 panels 20" (50.8 cm) wide x 30" (76.2 cm) long

Lining Fabric

Use the Main Panel Pattern piece provided.

Cut 2 Main Panels on the fold*.

Using a ruler and fabric marker, measure and mark the dimensions following directly on the **right** side of the fabric. Then cut along the marked lines.

Cut 1 Cell Phone Pocket Panel 5" (12.7 cm) wide x 10½" (26.7 cm) long

Fusible Interfacing*

Use the Lining Main Panels you just cut as a pattern piece.

Cut 4 Main Panels

Use the Cell Phone Pocket Panel you just cut and fold in half, matching the short ends; use this as a pattern piece.

Cut 1 Cell Phone Pocket

 Make the Exterior Patchwork Panels

a. Fold the first muslin panel in half, matching the short ends. Gently press a center crease.

b. Open the panel. Place the Main Panel pattern piece on the muslin with the center fold straight edge against the center crease and pin in place. Using your chalk pencil or marking pen, draw around the outside of the pattern piece. Remove the pins and flip the pattern piece to the other side of the center crease. The pattern piece will be face down. Draw around the outside edge to complete the outline.

c. Using a ruler and chalk pencil, measure 6½" (16.5 cm) down from the top edge of the outline along the center crease and make a mark. Draw a line perpendicular to the center crease at this mark across the panel.

d. Place the **wrong** side of the first Center Square onto the muslin, lining up the top and bottom points with the center crease and the left and right points with the drawn line, and pin in place.

e. Choose a 1¾" (4.4 cm) wide coordinating strip and cut an 8½" (21.6 cm) length. Lay the strip along the top right edge of the Center Square, **right** sides together, matching the raw edges, and pin through all layers. Stitch a ¼" (0.6 cm) seam along the pinned edge. Open the strip so the **right** side is up and press flat along the seam you just sewed, being careful not to form a pleat. Then pin the raw edges of the strip to the muslin.

f. Use your ruler and measure the top left edge of the Center Square and the short end of the strip you just attached. Select a second 1¾" (4.4 cm) coordinating strip and trim it to the length you just measured. Lay the strip along the top left edge of the square and strip, **right** sides together, matching the raw edges, and pin through all layers. Stitch a ¼" (0.6 cm)

seam along the pinned edge. Open the strip and press flat along the seam you just sewed. Then pin the raw edges of the strip to the muslin.

g. Continue this method of piecing and pressing with two more 1¾" (4.4 cm) coordinating strips on the lower left and lower **right** sides of the Center Square, using a ¼" (0.6 cm) seam.

h. Next, select four 2¼" (5.7 cm) coordinating strips and repeat this piecing and pressing to add another row around the Center Square. Start at the top right-hand side and work in a counterclockwise direction.

i. Now, alternate between the 1¾" (4.4 cm) and 2¼" (5.7 cm) strips, sewing additional rows around the panel, covering all the muslin inside the marked outline and extending the strips at least ½" (1.3 cm) past the drawn lines. (See Figure 1.)

Figure 1

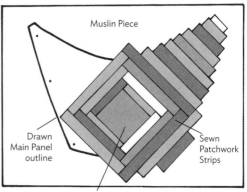

Muslin Piece

Drawn Main Panel outline

Sewn Patchwork Strips

Center Square on Point

j. Fold the pieced panel in half, **wrong** sides together, along the center crease. Use the Main Panel pattern piece to cut one Exterior Patchwork Panel, centering the pattern piece over the Center Square.

k. Open the Panel and machine baste* a ⅜" (1 cm) seam around all edges.

l. Repeat Steps 3a to 3k to make a second Exterior Patchwork Panel.

 Apply the Interfacing to the Exterior and Lining Panels

Tip: Follow the manufacturer's instructions closely when applying the fusible interfacing. If you experience any puckering of the fabric, gently pull back the interfacing while it is still warm and reapply.

Place the fusible side of one interfacing Main Panel on the **wrong** side of the first Exterior Patchwork Panel and fuse the interfacing to the panel. Repeat to apply the remaining interfacing Main Panels to the second Exterior Panel and the Lining Panels. Then fuse the one half of the Cell Phone Pocket interfacing piece to the **wrong** side of half the Cell Phone Pocket.

Transfer the Dots and Placement Lines

a. Use your chalk pencil and tracing paper to transfer Dots* A, B, and C from the Main Panel Pattern piece onto the interfaced sides of both the Exterior Patchwork and Lining Panels.

b. Transfer the Cell Phone Pocket placement lines from the Main Panel Pattern piece onto the **right** side of one of the Lining Panels.

Make the Gussets*

a. Fold the first corner of one Exterior Patchwork Panel at Dot C, **right** sides together, matching the side and bottom edges, and pin to hold in place.

b. Using your ruler and chalk pencil, measure and mark ½" (1.3 cm) in from Dot C. Then, measure 1½" (3.8 cm) from Dot C along the folded edge. Connect the two marks by drawing a line, continuing the line into the ½" (1.3 cm) seam allowance. (See Figure 2.)

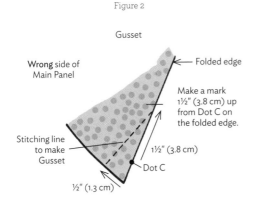

Figure 2

Gusset

Wrong side of Main Panel

Folded edge

Make a mark 1½" (3.8 cm) up from Dot C on the folded edge.

Stitching line to make Gusset

1½" (3.8 cm)

Dot C

½" (1.3 cm)

c. Stitch through all layers along this marked line.

d. Repeat Steps 6a to 6c on the second corner of the first Exterior Patchwork Panel, both corners of the second Exterior Patchwork Panel, and all corners of the Lining Panels.

Cover the Cording for the Bottom of the Bag

a. To sew the 2⅛" (5.4 cm) bias strips together into one long continuous piece, start by placing two strips perpendicular to each other **right** sides together, matching two short ends, and pin them in place. Stitch a ¼" (0.6 cm) seam across the pinned edges. Press the seam allowances open. Repeat until you've

sewn all of the bias strips into one long strip measuring at least 37" (94 cm).

b. Wrap the **wrong** side of this bias strip around 38" (96.5 cm) of the cotton cording, matching the long edges, and pin them together with **right** side out. Use the zipper foot and stitch a ⅜" (1 cm) seam from the matched edges to hold them in place.

Attach the Cording to One Exterior Patchwork Panel

Note: Continue to use the zipper/cording foot when stitching the cording to the Panel.

a. Place the covered cording on the **right** side of one Exterior Patchwork Panel, positioning one end at the first Dot B. Matching the raw edges, pin the cording along the bottom edge, bringing the other end up to the second Dot B. Ease the cording around the gussets.

b. Begin sewing ¾" (1.9 cm) below the first Dot B and stitch along the pinned edge until you are ¾" (1.9 cm) from the second Dot B.

c. Use your seam ripper and unstitch the fabric cover on the cording to where you stopped stitching, ¾" (1.9 cm) below the Dot B on both ends. Push the fabric out of the way and then cut the cording so that it is even with where you stopped stitching, ¾" (1.9 cm) below Dot B on both ends. Then, refold the fabric cover, extending the ends into the seam allowance up to Dot B to finish.

Sew the Exterior Patchwork Panels

Note: Continue to use your zipper foot when stitching the Exterior Patchwork Panels together.

a. Place the Exterior Patchwork Panels **right** sides together, matching the dots and gussets, and pin them in place.

b. Starting at the first Dot B, sew along the pinned edges down to the gusset, pivot*, continue sewing across the bottom to the next gusset, pivot again, and stitch up the other side of the bag, stopping at the second Dot B.

c. Press the seams open, then clip* the corners and turn **right** side out.

Make and Attach the Cell Phone Pocket

a. Replace the zipper foot with your standard foot. Fold the Cell Phone Pocket piece in half with the **right** sides together, matching the short ends, then pin around the raw edges. Stitch along the pinned edges, leaving a 3" (7.6 cm) opening centered along the short end (top).

b. Trim all four corners of the seam allowance, being careful not to clip your stitches.

c. Turn the pocket **right** side out and use a turning tool* to gently push out each corner. Fold each side of the opening ½" (1.3 cm) under, to the inside, and press the whole pocket flat. Pin the opening edges together.

d. Choose one side of the pocket to be the **right** side. Edge stitch* across the pinned edge to close the opening with the **right** side facing up. Then, topstitch* a second row of stitching ⅜" (1 cm) from the edge stitching line. Press.

e. Make a pleat at the bottom of the pocket by folding it in half lengthwise, **right** sides together. Match the side edges and pin them together. Starting at the bottom, sew ⅜" (1 cm) from the folded edge, stitching 1" (2.5 cm) in length.

f. Open the Cell Phone Pocket so the **wrong** side is facing up. Center the pleat evenly over the seam and press it flat.

g. Now place the **wrong** side of the Cell Phone Pocket onto the **right** side of the marked Lining Panel. Match the side and bottom edges with the placement lines and pin them in place. Edge stitch along the pinned edges.

 Complete the Lining

Repeat Steps 9a to 9c to sew the Lining Panels, but leave an 8" (20 cm) opening along the bottom edge for turning the bag **right** side out. Keep the lining turned **wrong** side out.

 Sew the Exterior and Lining Panels Together

a. With the Exterior **right** side out and the Lining **wrong** side out, slip the Lining over the Exterior with the **right** sides together.

b. Match and pin the edges between Dots A and B on each side and on each end of the bag. You will have four pinned sections. (See Figure 3.)

Figure 3

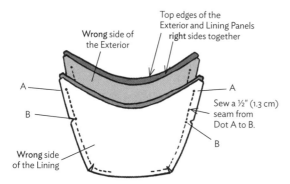

Wrong side of the Exterior

Top edges of the Exterior and Lining Panels right sides together

A

A

B

Sew a ½" (1.3 cm) seam from Dot A to B.

B

Wrong side of the Lining

c. Starting at one of the pinned sections, stitch from Dot A to Dot B. Clip into the seam allowances at Dot B, being careful not to clip the stitches. Repeat the stitching between Dots A and B on the three remaining sections, clipping at each Dot B.

d. Then, at each section, press the seam allowances open from Dot B up to the raw edges above Dot A.

e. Pin the seam allowances above Dot A to the Exterior and Lining Panels on all four sections and then edge stitch close to these pinned edges. (See Figure 4.) This will finish the areas that will become the Strap openings.

f. With the Exterior still inside the Lining, match the top edges on both sides of the bag, **right** sides together, and pin them in place.

g. Starting on one side of the bag, sew from one end of the top edge across to the other. Repeat this sewing on the opposite top edge. There will now be openings between Dot A and the top edge stitching on all four corners for the Straps. (See Figure 4.)

Figure 4

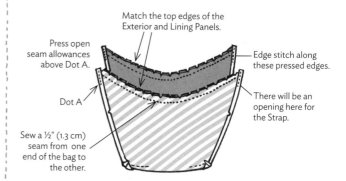

Match the top edges of the Exterior and Lining Panels.

Press open seam allowances above Dot A.

Edge stitch along these pressed edges.

Dot A

There will be an opening here for the Strap.

Sew a ½" (1.3 cm) seam from one end of the bag to the other.

h. Press both seams open and then clip into the seam allowances every ¾" (1.9 cm) along the curved top edges, being careful not to clip your stitching.

i. Turn the bag **right** side out by pulling it through the opening in the bottom of the Lining. Using a threaded hand-sewing needle, slipstitch* the opening closed and push the Lining down inside the Exterior. Press flat along the finished top edges. (See Figure 5.)

Figure 5

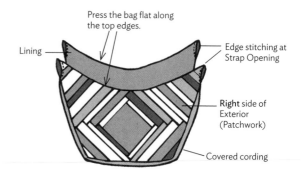

Press the bag flat along the top edges.

Lining

Edge stitching at Strap Opening

Right side of Exterior (Patchwork)

Covered cording

Sew the Strap Channels

a. Starting at one end of one Exterior side of the bag, using your ruler and chalk pencil, measure down from the top edge 1¼" (3.2 cm) and make a mark. Continue to move the ruler across the top edge, measuring down 1¼" (3.2 cm) and marking. Use your chalk pencil to connect these marks and lightly draw a line from one side end to the other side end.

b. Repeat this measuring and marking on the second side of the bag. These will be the topstitching lines for your Strap Channels.

c. Pin the Exterior to the Lining at these lines to keep the layers from shifting.

d. Starting on one side of the bag, stitch from one end to the other following the drawn line. Repeat the topstitching on the other side of the bag and then press along the stitching lines.

Make the Straps

a. Using the method described in Step 7a, sew the 3½" (8.9 cm) bias strips together to make two long continuous pieces at least 38" (96.5 cm) long each for the Strap Covers.

b. Fold the first Strap Cover in half lengthwise **wrong** sides together, and press a crease along the folded edge.

c. Open the Strap Cover and fold each long edge in toward the center crease and press. Sew a basting* stitch along each side of the center crease. This will hold the seam allowance in place when you insert the cording.

d. Fold the Strap Cover in half again at the center crease, enclosing the raw edges, and press. Pin along the matched folded edges.

e. Starting and stopping 3" (7.6 cm) from the ends, edge stitch the pinned folded edges together.

f. Cut a piece of cording 40" (101.6 cm) long. Wrap masking tape around both cut ends so that the cording holds its shape and doesn't fray.

g. Thread your large-eye hand-sewing needle with a double strand of carpet/button thread and make a knot at the ends. Push the needle through one end of the cording just below the tape. Stitch in place a couple of times to secure and then wrap the thread tightly around the cording below the tape so that there is a ½" (1.3 cm) thread band. Push the needle back and forth through the cording a couple of times and knot to secure and cut the thread.

h. Attach a large safety pin to the wrapped end of the cording and feed it into one Strap Cover opening, guiding it through until it comes out the opposite end and both ends of the cording are accessible. Remove the basting stitches on both sides of the Strap Cover's center crease.

i. Attach the safety pin through the wrapped edge of cording and the Strap Cover and feed the Strap into one Strap Opening, guiding it through until it comes out the opposite end and both ends are accessible. Check to make sure the Strap is not twisted in the channel and straighten it if necessary. Open the folds and bring the unstitched ends of the Straps together, with **right** sides facing, and pin to hold them in place. Stitch the two ends of the Straps together on your sewing machine, being careful not to catch the cording. Press the seam allowances open.

j. Cut the tape from the wrapped end of the cord, being careful not to cut the thread wrapping. Lay the Strap on a flat surface so the Strap is positioned in a circle. Arrange the ends of the cording within the Strap Cover so that the thread wrapped end is overlapped by the taped end and the cording fills the Strap without stretching the cover. Use your fabric marker and mark the second end of the cording where the ends intersect.

k. Repeat Step 14g to wrap the second end of the cording below the mark, but do not cut the thread. Cut away the cording above the mark, being careful not to the cut the thread wrapping.

l. Place the two ends of the cording so that they butt together. Use the attached needle and thread and sew back and forth across the wrapped ends to attach them together. Knot and cut the thread. Do not sew through the Strap Cover.

m. Refold the opening in the Strap Cover, tucking the seam allowances and cording into the fold. Pin the opening closed and then hand stitch to secure.

n. Repeat Steps 14b through 14m, to make and insert the second Strap.

o. Rotate both Straps in their channels until the sewn ends are hidden inside.

Tribal Cuffs

Finished sizes: Cuff #1: 2⅜" (6 cm) wide x 8½" (21.6 cm) long • Cuff #2: 2" (5.1 cm) wide x 8½" (21.6 cm) long

Modern and chic with very high style points, these fashionable cuffs add just the right pop of color to your wardrobe!

NOTES

All seams are ¼" (0.6 cm) unless otherwise stated. The seam allowance is included in all measurements.

DESIGN INFLUENCES

Triangles
Stripes
Flying Geese

TECHNIQUES USED

Paper Piecing
Appliqué
Hand Embroidery
Beadwork

Figure 1

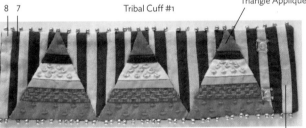

Tribal Cuff #1

Triangle Appliqué

8 7

Cuff Base

Tribal Cuff 1

MATERIALS LIST

Fabrics

Note: I used small amounts of yardage in my studio to create this cuff, but if you have small scraps of fabric that you have been saving, this is a great project to use them and give them a chance to shine!

From 44" (112 cm) wide light- to mid-weight fabric
⅛ yard (0.11 m) of light colored solid for the Cuff Base
⅛ yard (0.11 m) of dark colored solid for the Cuff Base
⅛ yard (0.11 m) each of 6 coordinating solids or prints for the Triangle Appliqués
⅛ yard (0.11 m) of coordinating solid or print for the Cuff Backing

OTHER SUPPLIES

⅛ yard (0.11 m) of 20" (50.8 cm) wide fusible knit interfacing (Pellon EK130)
2 or 3 sheets of foundation paper, measuring 8½" x 11" (21.6 cm x 27.9 cm) (Carol Doak's)
1 spool of coordinating all-purpose thread (Coats)
1 spool of 50-weight cotton embroidery thread in a neutral shade for the appliqué (Coats)
1 spool of transparent or beading thread (Coats)
1 skein of metallic silver embroidery floss or 1 spool of silver metallic thread (Coats)
2 skeins of coordinating embroidery floss (Coats)
75 (approximately) 3.4 mm fringe teardrop seed beads (Miyuki Beads)
2 transparent sew-on snaps ⁵⁄₁₆" (0.79 cm) (Prym Dritz Iron-Safe Clear Nylon Sewing Snaps)

ADDITIONAL TOOLS NEEDED

Ruler that works with rotary cutter and has 1/8" (0.3 cm) markings (such as an Add-An-Eighth Ruler)
1 hand-embroidery needle (size 5 or 7)
Turning tool (Prym-Dritz)
1 standard hand-sewing needle
1 milliner's needle (size 11) (Prym-Dritz)
1 beading needle (size 10) (Prym-Dritz)
Needle-nose pliers (optional)

 Cut Out the Template Pieces

From the pattern sheet included with this book, cut out:
Cuff Base Template
Triangle Template

 Cut Out the Fabric Pieces

Use your rotary cutter, mat, and ruler to cut the following pieces.

Triangle Appliqués

Lay out the 6 triangle appliqué fabrics in the order you wish to use them. Number the fabrics from 1 to 6, from bottom to top.

Cut 3 strips of Fabric 1 – 1" x 3" (2.5 x 7.6 cm)
Cut 3 strips of Fabric 2 – ⅞" x 3" (2.2 x 7.6 cm)
Cut 3 strips of Fabric 3 – ¾" x 3" (1.9 x 7.6 cm)
Cut 3 strips of Fabric 4 – 1" x 3" (2.5 x 7.6 cm)
Cut 3 strips of Fabric 5 – ¾" x 3" (1.9 x 7.6 cm)
Cut 3 strips of Fabric 6 – 1" x 3" (2.5 x 7.6 cm)

Cuff Base
Number the two contrasting fabrics 7 and 8.
Cut 15 strips of Fabric 8 – 1" x 3⅜" (2.5 x 8.6 cm)
Cut 12 strips of Fabric 7 – 1" x 3⅜" (2.5 x 8.6 cm)
Cut 3 strips of Fabric 7 – 1¼" x 3⅜" (3.2 x 8.6 cm)

Cuff Backing
Cut 1 piece – 9½" x 3⅜" (24.1 x 8.6 cm)

Interfacing
Cut 1 piece – 9½" x 3⅜" (24.1 x 8.6 cm)

Foundation Paper
Cut 3 pieces – 5" x 5" (12.7 x 12.7 cm)
Cut 1 piece – 12" x 5" (30.5 x 12.7 cm)

Paper Piece the Cuff Base
Note: The fabric strips shown in the following images (Figures 2 to 5) extend past the top and bottom edges of the template for illustration purposes only. When you sew them together in the following steps, they will be the same height as the template.

a. Trace the Cuff Base Template onto one of the sheets of foundation paper, making sure your lines are straight, as you will be following these lines when you are stitching. Transfer the numbers onto each section.

b. Place one Fabric 8 piece vertically, **wrong** side up, on a flat surface. Next, take one Fabric 7 piece that measures 1" x 3⅜" (2.5 x 8.6 cm) and place it vertically under the Fabric 8 piece so that **right** sides are together and top and bottom edges line up. Place the foundation paper from Step 3a on top with the drawn side facing you. One long side of the Fabric Piece 8 needs to line up with the edge of the template and the other long side should extend a ¼" (0.6 cm) into Section 2. Pin the layers together through the paper with the paper on top. Make sure all of the edges of the fabrics line up.

c. Reduce the stitch length on your sewing machine to 1.5 (12 to 14 stitches/inch/2.5 cm). With the paper side up, stitch along the drawn line between Sections 1 and 2, stitching slightly past the beginning and the end of the line.

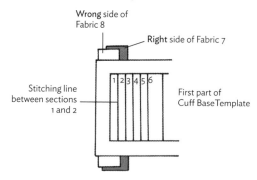

Figure 2

Wrong side of Fabric 8

Right side of Fabric 7

Stitching line between sections 1 and 2

First part of Cuff Base Template

d. Fold the paper back along this stitched line. Use your ruler, rotary cutter, and mat and trim the seam allowance* under Section 2 to ⅛" (0.3 cm).

e. Flip the paper over and press the fabrics pieces open, making sure to press along the seam with the seam allowances to one side. Fabric 7 will now be under Section 2 and will extend ¼" (0.6 cm) past the line between Sections 2 and 3. (See Figure 3.)

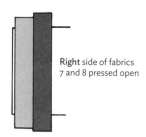

Figure 3

Right side of fabrics 7 and 8 pressed open

f. Pin a second Fabric 8 piece, **right** sides together, with the pressed open Fabric 7 piece, matching the raw edges. With the paper side up, stitch along the drawn line between Sections 2 and 3, stitching slightly past the beginning and the end of the line. Repeat Steps 3d and 3e. Fabric 8 will now be under Section 3 and will extend past the line between Sections 3 and 4. (See Figure 4.)

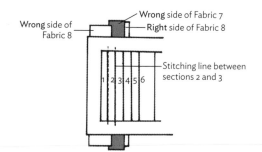

Figure 4

Wrong side of Fabric 8

Wrong side of Fabric 7

Right side of Fabric 8

Stitching line between sections 2 and 3

g. Continue on with this method of sewing, trimming, and pressing, as you work in numerical order, alternating between the 1" x 3⅜" (2.5 x 8.6 cm) strips of Fabrics 7 and 8, until you have five strips. The fifth strip will be Fabric 8.

h. Now, add a wider (1¼" x 3⅜" [3.2 x 8.6 cm]) Fabric 7 strip, using the same method. Continue alternating the narrower strips. The thirteenth strip will be Fabric 8.

i. Repeat Step 3h so that the second wide Fabric 7 strip will be under Section 14 and seven more narrow strips follow.

j. Add the last wide Fabric 7 strip under Section 22, then connect the remaining six strips in the same way to finish piecing the Cuff Base.

k. Gently remove the paper from the **wrong** side of the Cuff Base. It should measure 9½" (24.1 cm) wide x 3⅜" (8.6 cm) tall.

 Paper Piece the Triangles

Note: Refer to Figures 2 to 4 as a guide for paper piecing the Triangles.

a. Trace the Triangle Template onto each of the three 5" (12.7 cm) square sheets of foundation paper, making sure your lines are straight, as you will be following these lines when you are stitching. Transfer the numbers onto each section of each Triangle tracing.

b. Start to paper piece the first Triangle by using the same method in Step 3, sewing, trimming, and pressing the pieces and working in numerical order, ending with Fabric 6 covering all of the sections.

c. Do not remove the paper. It will act as a stabilizer for the hand embroidery.

d. Repeat for the remaining two Triangles.

 Embroider the Triangles

Note: I chose to embroider three of the strips in each Triangle with a running stitch* and a cross stitch, but other hand embroidery stitches can be used.

a. Follow the guide for the embroidery designs in Figure 5 and make the stitch marks on the **right** side of each Triangle with a chalk pencil or fabric marker.

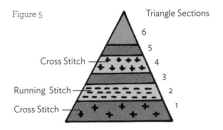

Figure 5

Triangle Sections

6
5
Cross Stitch — 4
3
Running Stitch — 2
Cross Stitch — 1

b. Thread your hand embroidery needle with three strands of floss. Tie a knot at one end.

c. Beginning and ending on the **wrong** side, use the traced lines as a guide to embroider with a running stitch on the Fabric Strip 2. Knot the embroidery floss on the **wrong** side of the Triangle with the last stitch.

d. On Fabric Strips 1 and 4, beginning and ending on the **wrong** side, follow the marked lines as a guide and embroider cross stitches on Fabric Strips 1 and 4. Start by making a single straight stitch about ⅛" to ³⁄₁₆" (0.3 to 0.5 cm) long, taking the needle back into the fabric to the **wrong** side. Then bring the needle back through to the **right** side and cross over the original stitch. Repeat for the other marks, staggering the crosses in each row and knotting the embroidery floss on the **wrong** side of the Triangle with each stitch.

e. Cut the Triangle along the outside edge of the template. You can gently remove the paper backing or leave it in place.

 Sew the Cuff Base to the Backing

a. Fuse the piece of knit interfacing to the **wrong** side of the Cuff Base.

b. Pin the Cuff Base and the Backing **right** sides together, matching all edges. Stitch together using a ½" (1.3 cm) seam allowance, pivoting* at each corner and leaving a 1½" (3.8 cm) opening at one short end for turning the Cuff. Trim the seam allowances to ¼" (0.6 cm) and trim the corners*.

c. Turn the Cuff **right** side out, gently pushing out the corners with a turning tool. Then press well along the seams, turning under the seam allowances on the open end to the inside of the Cuff.

d. Using a hand needle and thread, slipstitch* the opening closed.

 Appliqué the Triangles

a. Stay stitch* ¼" (0.6 cm) from all sides of each Triangle. Snip the points of the Triangles, leaving at least ⅛" (0.3 cm) seam allowance. Then turn the edges to the **wrong** side along this stitched line and press.

b. Pin each Triangle to the Cuff so that the tip of the Triangle is centered in the middle of a wide Fabric 7 section and the base is even with the bottom sewn edge of the Cuff. (See Figure 1.)

c. Thread the milliner's needle with a double strand of cotton embroidery thread and tie a knot. Hide the knot under each appliqué as you start and end your stitching.

d. Start at the top of the Triangle. Make sure the edges are folded under while you stitch, especially at the points. Take a couple of tiny stitches at the point and then, using an appliqué stitch*, sew down one side, catching only the Cuff Base and not stitching through to the Backing. When you reach the next point, follow the same steps and take a couple of tiny stitches at that point and then turn down the other side. Continue stitching all three sides and then hide a knot under the appliqué at the top.

e. Repeat for the remaining two Triangles.

8 Finish the Cuff

a. Thread your beading needle with a double strand of transparent thread and tie a knot at the end. Tip: Kink the thread with a pair of needle-nose pliers where you want the knot to go. When you tie the knot at this kink, it will be less likely to shift. Use the pliers to help pull the knot tight.

b. Hand stitch the silver beads to both long edges of the Cuff, spacing the beads about ³⁄₁₆" to ¼" (0.5 to 0.6 cm) apart and hiding the stitching and the knots in the seams.

c. Try the Cuff on to mark the position of the snaps with a chalk pencil. Use a double strand of transparent thread and a hand-sewing needle to sew the clear snaps to each mark.

Tribal Cuff 2

Figure 6

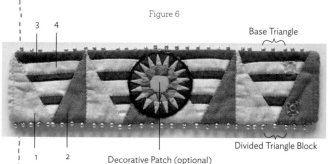

Base Triangle

3 4

1 2

Decorative Patch (optional)

Divided Triangle Block

MATERIALS LIST

Fabrics

Note: I used small amounts of yardage in my studio to create this cuff, but if you have small scraps of fabric that you have been saving, this is a great project to use them and give them a chance to shine!

From 44" (112 cm) wide light- to mid-weight fabric
⅛ yard (0.11 m) of light colored solid for the Divided Triangle
⅛ yard (0.11 m) of dark colored solid for the Divided Triangle
⅛ yard (0.11 m) each of 2 contrasting solids or prints for the Base Triangle
⅛ yard (0.11 m) of coordinating solid or print for the Cuff Backing

OTHER SUPPLIES

1 decorative patch or vintage pin, about 1¾" (4.5 cm) diameter (optional)
⅛ yard (0.11 m) of 45" (114.3 cm) wide fusible fleece (Pellon 987F)
4 sheets of foundation paper 8½" x 11" (21.6 x 27.9 cm) (Carol Doak's)
1 spool of coordinating all-purpose thread (Coats)
1 spool of 50-weight cotton embroidery thread in a neutral shade for the appliqué
1 spool of transparent or beading thread (Coats)
1 spool of silver metallic thread (Coats)
75 (approximately) 3.4 mm fringe teardrop seed beads (Miyuki Beads)
2 transparent sew-on snaps ⁵⁄₁₆" (7 mm) (Prym Dritz Iron-Safe Clear Nylon Sewing Snaps)

ADDITIONAL TOOLS NEEDED

Ruler that works with rotary cutter and has ⅛" (0.3 cm) markings (such as an Add-An-Eighth Ruler)
Turning tool
1 standard hand-sewing needle
1 milliner's needle (size 11)
1 beading needle (size 10)
Needle-nose pliers (optional)
Metallic needle for your sewing machine (optional)
Sewer's Aid thread lubricant (Dritz) (optional)

1 Cut Out the Template Pieces

From the pattern sheet included with this book, cut out:
Base Triangle Template
Divided Triangle Template

2 Cut Out the Fabric Pieces

Use your rotary cutter, mat, and ruler to cut the following specific amounts.

Divided Triangles

Number the fabrics 1 and 2.
Cut 4 pieces of Fabric 1 – 3¼" x 3"(8.3 x 7.6 cm)
Cut 4 pieces of Fabric 2 – 3¼" x 3" (8.3 x 7.6 cm)

Base Triangles

Number the two contrasting fabrics 3 and 4.
Cut 12 strips of Fabric 3 – 1" x 3¼" (2.5 x 8.3 cm)
Cut 8 strips of Fabric 4 – 1" x 3¼" (2.5 x 8.3 cm)
Cut 4 strips of Fabric 4 – 1⅜" x 3¼" (3.5 x 8.3 cm)

Cuff Backing

Cut 1 piece – 9½" x 3" (24.1 x 7.6 cm)

Fusible Fleece

Cut 1 piece – 9½" x 3" (24.1 x 7.6 cm)

Foundation Paper

Cut 8 pieces – 5" (12.7 cm) square

3 Paper Piece the Base Triangles

Note: Refer to Figures 2 to 5 in Tribal Cuff 1 as a guide for paper piecing the Base Triangles.

a. Trace the Base Triangle template onto four of the squares of foundation paper, making sure your lines are straight, as you will be following these lines when you are stitching. Transfer the numbers onto each section of each template tracing.

b. Place the **wrong** side of one Fabric 3 piece under Section 1 on the undrawn side of the paper at the base of the triangle, matching one long and both short edges along the bottom and sides of the template. The other long edge of the fabric piece needs to extend ¼" (0.6 cm) past the line between Sections 1 and 2. Then take one 1" (2.5 cm) wide Fabric 4 piece and match it with the Fabric 3 piece **right** sides together. Pin these layers together through the paper with the paper on top.

c. Reduce the stitch length on your sewing machine to 1.5 (12 to 14 stitches/inch/2.5 cm). With the paper side up, stitch along the drawn line between Sections 1 and 2, stitching slightly past the beginning and the end of the line.

d. Fold the paper back along this stitched line. Use your ruler, rotary cutter, and mat, and trim the seam allowance to ⅛" (0.3 cm).

e. Flip the paper over and press the fabrics open, making sure to press along the seam with the seam allowance staying in one direction. Fabric 4 will now be under Section 2 and will extend past the line between Sections 2 and 3.

f. Pin a second Fabric 3 piece **right** sides together with the pressed open Fabric 4 piece, matching the raw edges, so that both pieces are under Section 2. With the paper side up, stitch along the drawn line between Sections 2 and 3, stitching slightly past the beginning and the end of the line. Repeat Steps 3d and 3e. Fabric 3 will now be under Section 3 and will extend past the line between Sections 3 and 4.

g. Continue on with this method of sewing, trimming, and pressing, working in numerical order and alternating between Fabrics 3 and 4, until you have covered all the sections. Note that you will use a wider (1⅜" x 3¼" [3.5 x 8.3 cm]) Fabric 4 piece for Section 6.

h. Repeat these steps for the other three Base Triangles. Gently remove the paper from the back.

4 Attaching the Divided Triangles

a. Trace the Divided Triangle Template onto four separate sheets of 5" (12.7 cm) square foundation paper, making sure your lines are straight, as you will be following these lines when you are stitching. Transfer the numbers onto each section of each template tracing.

b. Place the **wrong** side of one Base Triangle against the undrawn side of the first traced template.

c. Next, place one Fabric 1 piece under the Base Triangle so the **right** sides are together, matching the edges. Pin through all three layers with the paper on top.

d. Sew along the line between Sections 1 and 2 with the paper side up. Stitch slightly past the beginning and end of the line. (See Figure 7.)

Note: The fabric in the image is shown slightly smaller for illustration purposes only.

Figure 7

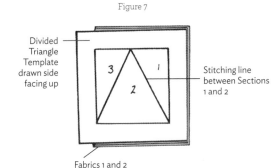

Divided Triangle Template drawn side facing up

Stitching line between Sections 1 and 2

Fabrics 1 and 2

e. Fold the paper back along this stitched line. Use your ruler, rotary cutter, and mat and trim the seam allowance to ⅛" (0.3 cm). Flip the piece over and press the fabrics open, making sure to press along the seam. (See Figure 8.)

Figure 8

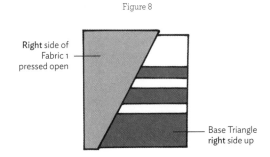

Right side of Fabric 1 pressed open

Base Triangle right side up

f. Now place one Fabric 2 piece under the Base Triangle **right** sides together, matching all of the edges. Pin through all three layers with the paper on top.

g. Sew along the line between sections 2 and 3 with the paper side up. Stitch slightly past the beginning and end of the line.

h. Fold the paper back along this stitched line. Use your ruler, mat, and rotary cutter to trim the seam allowance to ⅛" (0.3 cm). Turn the piece over and press the fabrics open, making sure to press along the seam. (See Figure 9.)

Figure 9

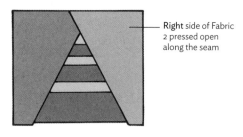

 Right side of Fabric 2 pressed open along the seam

i. Repeat Steps 4b to 4h for the remaining three Divided Triangles and Bases.

j. Trim along the outside edges of the template and gently remove the paper from the **wrong** side.

 Make the Cuff

a. Pin the Divided Triangle blocks together, aligning the Fabric 1 edges with the Fabric 2 edges and carefully matching the points. Sew with a ½" (1.3 cm) seam allowance. Trim the seams to ¼" (0.6 cm) and press open.

b. The Cuff will measure 9½" x 3" (24.1 x 7.6 cm). Make sure all of the paper has been removed from the **wrong** side.

 Quilt the Cuff

a. Follow the manufacturer's instructions and apply the fusible fleece to the **wrong** side of the Cuff.

b. Next, thread your sewing machine with the metallic thread through your needle and the 50-weight cotton embroidery thread in your bobbin. Increase your stitch length to 3.0 (10 stitches/inch/2.5 cm) Tips: When working with metallic thread, decrease the top tension on your machine if necessary. Apply a thread lubricant like Sewer's-Aid to the thread and use a needle specially made for metallics. Make sure your thread is not twisting as it is unwinding off of the thread spool.

c. Stitch-in-the-ditch* along all of the seams through all of the layers.

 Sew the Cuff to the Backing

a. Pin the Cuff and the Backing **right** sides together, matching all edges. Stitch the pieces together using a ½" (1.3 cm) seam allowance, pivoting at each corner and leaving a 1" (2.5

cm) opening at one short end for turning the Cuff. Trim the seam allowances to ¼" (0.6 cm) and clip* the corners.

b. Turn the Cuff **right** side out, gently pushing out the corners with a turning tool. Press well along the seams; turn under the seam allowances on the open end to the inside of the Cuff and press.

c. Using a hand-sewing needle and thread, slipstitch the opening closed.

8 Finish the Cuff

a. Center the appliqué piece over the middle Divided Triangle and pin in place.

b. Thread the milliner's needle with a double strand of cotton embroidery thread and tie a knot. Hide the knot under the appliqué as you start and end your stitching.

c. Take a couple of tiny stitches at the beginning and then, using an appliqué stitch, sew around the outside edge of the appliqué, catching only the top layer of the Cuff and not stitching through to the Back.

d. Thread your beading needle with a double strand of transparent thread and tie a knot at the end. Tip: Kink the thread with a pair of needle-nose pliers where you want the knot to go. When you tie the knot at this kink, it will be less likely to shift. Use the pliers to help pull the knot tight.

e. Hand stitch the silver beads to both long edges of the Cuff, spacing the beads about ³⁄₁₆" to ¼" (0.5 to 0.6 cm) apart and hiding the stitching in the seam.

f. Try the Cuff on and mark the position of the snaps with a chalk pencil. Use a double strand of transparent thread and a hand-sewing needle to sew the clear snaps to each mark.

Stash Pouches

Finished sizes: Large – 10" (25.4 cm) wide x 8½" (21.6 cm) tall x 3½" (8.9 cm) deep

Medium – 9" (22.9 cm) wide x 7" (17.8 cm) tall x 3" (7.6 cm) deep • Small – 8" (20.3 cm) wide x 6" (15.2 cm) tall x 3" (7.6 cm) deep

Stash cosmetics, office and art supplies, travel gear, and tech devices in these pouches.
We all need pretty storage for our personal bits to keep us organized and looking good!

NOTES

All seams are ½" (1.3 cm) unless otherwise stated. The seam
allowance is included in all measurements.

DESIGN INFLUENCE

Flying Geese

TECHNIQUE USED

Paper Piecing

Figure 1

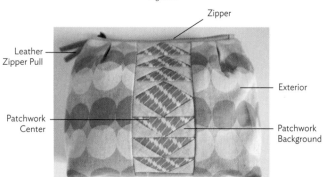

- Zipper
- Leather Zipper Pull
- Exterior
- Patchwork Center
- Patchwork Background

MATERIALS LIST

Note: Yardage and supplies listed are for all three bags.

Fabrics

Use Figure 1 as a guide
From 44" (112 cm) wide light- to mid-weight fabric
1 yard (0.91 m) of linen print for Exterior
⅛ yard (0.11 m) of cotton print for Patchwork Center
¼ yard (0.23 m) of linen solid for Patchwork Background
1 yard (0.91 m) of linen for Lining

OTHER SUPPLIES

1 piece of soft, dyed leather measuring around 3" x 8" (7.6 x 20.3 cm)
3⅝ yards (3.31 m) of 20" (50.8 cm) wide fusible woven interfacing
   (Pellon SF101)

⅛ yard (0.11 m) of 40" (101.6 cm) wide fusible fleece (Pellon 987F)
3 metal zippers at least the given size: Large – 12" (30.5 cm);
   Medium – 10" (25.4 cm); Small – 8" (20.3 cm) (Note: To achieve the
   look I wanted for the Pouches, I used a 35" [88.9 cm] antique brass
   zipper, cut it into three lengths, and added the bell pull sliders.)
3 antique brass bell pull sliders (Optional: The bell pull sliders provide
   a larger eye for the leather zipper pull.)
3 sheets of foundation paper 9" x 12" (22.9 x 30.5 cm) (Carol Doak's)
1 spool of transparent thread
1 spool of coordinating all-purpose thread

ADDITIONAL TOOLS NEEDED

Ruler that works with rotary cutter and has ¼" (0.6 cm) markings
   (such as an Add-A-Quarter Ruler)
Zipper foot for your sewing machine
1 standard hand-sewing needle
Turning Tool

 Cut Out the Pattern Pieces

From the pattern sheet included with this book, cut out:
Patchwork Template for Stash Pouch-Small
Patchwork Template for Stash Pouch-Medium
Patchwork Template for Stash Pouch-Large
Small Pouch
Stash Pouch-Small Lining
Medium Pouch
Stash Pouch-Medium Lining
Large Pouch
Stash Pouch-Large Lining

 Cut Out the Fabric Pieces

Exterior Print
For the Large Pouch cut:
1 Large Back on the fold*
2 Large Fronts (fold back pattern piece on indicated line)
1 Large Patchwork Bottom – 4" (10.2 cm) wide x 2¾" (7.0 cm) long
1 Zipper End – 1½" (3.8 cm) square

For the Medium Pouch cut:

1 Medium Back on the fold

2 Medium Fronts (fold back pattern piece on indicated line)

1 Medium Patchwork Bottom – 3¾" (9.5 cm) wide x 2½" (6.4 cm) long

1 Zipper End – 1½" (3.8 cm) square

For the Small Pouch cut:

1 Small Back on the fold

2 Small Fronts (fold back pattern piece on indicated line)

1 Small Patchwork Bottom – 3½" (8.9 cm) wide x 2½" (6.4 cm) long

1 Zipper End – 1½" (3.8 cm) square

Patchwork Center Print

Cut 1 strip 4½" (11.4 cm) x width of fabric* (wof) (used in all three pouches)

Patchwork Background Solid

Cut 2 strips 4" (10.2 cm) x wof (used in all three pouches)

Lining

For the Large Pouch cut:

2 Large Lining on the fold

1 Pocket – 14½" (36.8 cm) wide x 13" (33 cm) long

For the Medium Pouch cut:

2 Medium Lining on the fold

1 Pocket – 13" (33 cm) wide x 11" (28 cm) long

For the Small Pouch cut:

2 Small Lining on the fold

1 Pocket – 12" (30.5 cm) wide x 9" (22.9 cm) long

Fusible Woven Interfacing

Use previously cut fabric pieces as templates.

For the Large Pouch cut:

1 Large Back

2 Large Fronts

2 Large Lining

1 Large Patchwork Bottom

For the Medium Pouch cut:

1 Medium Back

2 Medium Fronts

2 Medium Lining

1 Medium Patchwork Bottom

For the Small Pouch cut:

1 Small Back

2 Small Fronts

2 Small Lining

1 Small Patchwork Bottom

Fusible Fleece

For the Large Pouch cut:

1 Large Patchwork Backing – 3" (7.6 cm) wide x 8" (20.3 cm) long

For the Medium Pouch cut:

1 Medium Patchwork Backing – 2¾" (7 cm) wide x 7" (18 cm) long

For the Small Pouch cut:

1 Small Patchwork Backing – 2½" (6.4 cm) wide x 6" (15.2 cm) long

Leather Piece

Cut 3 pieces – ¼" (0.6 cm) wide x 7" (18 cm) long

Note: The instructions for the construction of the Large, Medium, and Small Pouches are the same. Use the cut pieces for the size you are making.

 Fuse Interfacing to Fabric Panels

Follow the manufacturer's instructions to fuse the interfacing pieces to their corresponding fabric panels.

Transfer Pleat Marks

Using your chalk pencil and ruler, transfer the pleat marks onto the **wrong** side of the Back (on both sides of the fold) and Front Panels.

 Make the Paper Pieced Patchwork Panel

a. Trace the Patchwork Template onto one of the foundation papers, making sure your lines are straight, as you will be following these lines when you are stitching. Transfer the numbers of each section onto the tracing.

b. Place the Patchwork Center (A1) and Patchwork Background (A2) strips **right** sides together with the Patchwork center strip on top, matching the short end raw edges.

c. Fold the paper foundation back, **right** sides together, along the diagonal line between A1 and A2. Position the paper onto the **wrong** side of the Patchwork Center so the raw short edge is ¼" (0.6 cm) above the paper fold, the strip is completely covering A1, and the ½" (1.3 cm) seam allowance is on the right-hand side of the foundation. Unfold the paper foundation and pin through the A1 section to keep the strips in place.

d. Shorten your stitch length to 1.5 and stitch along the line between A1 and A2. Start stitching a couple of stitch lengths before the line starts and continue the stitching line through the seam allowance. (See Figure 2.)

Figure 2

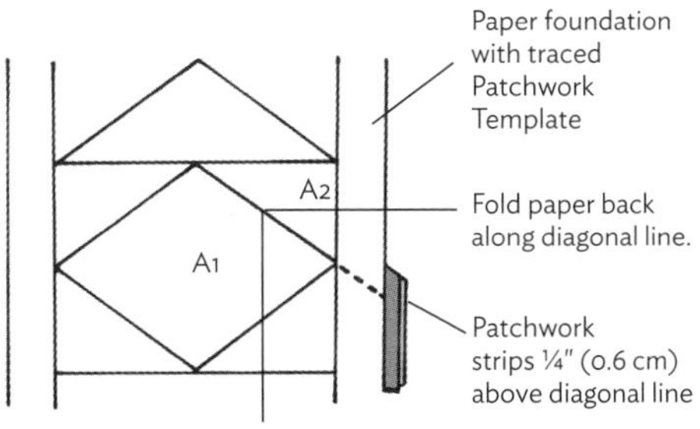

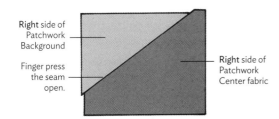

Stitching line between Sections A1 and A2

e. Flip the foundation so the fabric is up, open the fabric so it lies flat, and finger press* the seam open. (See Figure 3.)

Figure 3

Right side of Patchwork Background — Finger press the seam open. — Right side of Patchwork Center fabric

f. Flip so the paper side is up and check that the Patchwork Background strip covers Triangle A2 and the seam allowance is on the right-hand side. Trim away only the excess Center and Background strips so the fabric left covers the Diamond A1 and Triangle A2 by at least ½" (1.3 cm).

g. Fold the paper foundation back (the paper will rip a little around the stitches that extend at the beginning of the previous seam), **right** sides together, along the diagonal line between A1 and A3. Use your Add-A-Quarter ruler and trim the fabric beyond the fold to ¼" (0.6 cm).

h. Trim the short edge of the Background strip so that it has a straight edge. Place the foundation fabric side down, onto the **right** side of the Background strip, matching the edge beyond the fold with the short edge of the strip. Position it so the right-hand long edge of the Background strip is ⅜" (1 cm) beyond the right-hand end of the line and all of the ½" (1.3 cm) seam allowance on the left-hand side is covered. Unfold the paper foundation and pin through the Diamond A1 to keep the strips in place.

i. Stitch along the line between A1 and A3. Start stitching a couple of stitch lengths before the line starts and continue the stitching line through the seam allowance. (See Figure 4.)

Figure 4

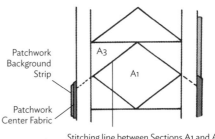

Patchwork Background Strip — Patchwork Center Fabric

Stitching line between Sections A1 and A3

j. Fold the paper foundation back (the paper will rip a little around the stitches that extend at the beginning of the previous seam) along the line between A1 and A3. Use your Add-A-Quarter ruler and trim the fabric beyond the fold to ¼" (0.6 cm).

k. Flip the foundation so the fabric is up, open the fabric so it lies flat, and finger press the seam. (See Figure 5.)

Figure 5

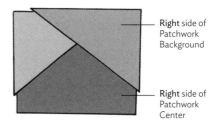

Right side of Patchwork Background — Right side of Patchwork Center

l. Flip so the paper foundation side is up and check that the Patchwork Background strip covers Triangle A3 and the seam allowance on the left-hand side. Trim away the excess Background strip so the fabric covers the Triangle A3 by at least ½" (1.3 cm).

m. Fold the foundation, **right** sides together, along the line at the bottom of Triangle A4. Trim the short edge of the Patchwork Center strip so it has a straight edge. Place the foundation fabric side down, on the **right** side of the Center strip, matching the edge beyond the fold with the short edge of the strip. Position it so the right- and left-hand long edges of the Center strip cover the side seam allowance of the foundation. Unfold the paper foundation and pin through Diamond A1 to keep the strips in place. Stitch along the line between A4 and A2/A3.

n. Continue in the same manner to complete the foundation piece.

o. Trim the completed foundation along the seam allowance line. Do not remove foundation paper yet.

 Make the Front Panel

a. Pin the Patchwork Panel and Patchwork Bottom with **right** sides together along the short ends. Sew along the pinned edge and press the seam allowance toward the Patchwork Bottom.

b. Align the Patchwork Panel and one Front Panel along the long straight edges, with **right** sides together. Sew together and press the seam allowance toward the Front Panel. Repeat with the second Front Panel on the opposite side of the Patchwork Panel.

c. Remove the foundation paper.

d. Follow the manufacturer's instructions to fuse fleece to the **wrong** side of the Patchwork Panel. Line up the bottom of the fleece with the Patchwork Panel/Patchwork Bottom seam. There will be a ½" (1.3 cm) at the top of the Patchwork Panel that will not be covered by fleece.

e. Put the transparent thread in your machine's needle and set the stitch length to 3.0. Then stitch-in-the-ditch* in all the seams of the Patchwork Panel.

 Make the Pleats

a. Fold the Front Panel **right** sides together, matching the first two pleat lines, and pin them in place. Stitch a ¾" (1.9 cm) seam vertically along the marked lines and backstitch* at each end.

b. Center the pleat evenly on each side of the seam and press flat. Machine baste* ⅜" (1 cm) from the top edge to hold in place.

c. Repeat Steps 7a and 7b to make the remaining pleat on the Front Panel and both pleats on the Back Panel.

Make the Pocket

a. Fold the Pocket in half lengthwise, with the **right** sides together. Pin and sew along the long edge.

b. Turn the Pocket **right** side out and press flat with the seam at the bottom. Topstitch* ¼" (0.6 cm) from the top folded edge.

c. Fold the Pocket in half, matching the short ends, and press to mark the center.

d. On one Lining Panel draw a line across the width of the Panel ⅝" (1.6 cm) above the cut-out corner.

e. Place the Pocket onto the **right** side of the Lining Panel, laying the bottom of the pocket along the line drawn, and pin. Edge stitch* through all layers along the bottom of the Pocket.

f. Trim the Pocket side edges to match the curve of the Lining. Machine baste ¼" (0.6 cm) along the side edges to hold the Pocket in place.

g. Topstitch along the center crease of the Pocket.

Attach the Zipper

Note: If you are cutting a longer zipper into smaller lengths, make sure to cut the zipper 2" (5.1 cm) longer than the required length. Then stitch a bartack* stitch across the zipper teeth at the base of the zipper 1" (2.5 cm) above the cut end to make a zipper stop. Slide the zipper pulls onto the top end of the zipper teeth. Open the top end of the teeth and sew a bartack 1" (2.5 cm) down from the top of each side of the teeth to keep the pull from sliding off.

a. Fold one Zipper End in half lengthwise **wrong** sides together and press a center crease, then open it up.

b. With the **wrong** side facing up, fold two raw edges in to meet at the center crease and press.

c. Fold it again at the center crease, enclosing the raw edges, and press.

d. Cut the zipper across the zipper teeth just above the metal (or bartack) stopper. Slide the Zipper into the Zipper End so it nestles against the center fold and pin in place. Note: The Zipper End will be wider than the Zipper.

e. Edge stitch along the top folded edge of the Zipper End, making sure you catch both the folded edges on the front and back of the zipper. Tip: When sewing across the metal teeth of the zipper slow down or walk your machine needle to prevent needle breakage.

f. Trim the Zipper End even with the zipper sides.

g. Using your chalk pencil and ruler, measure and mark the placement for the bottom of the zipper along the ½" (1.3 cm) seam line at the top of the Front Panel, ⅝" (1.6 cm) from the right-hand edge. Then place the Back Panel with the **right** side facing up and measure and mark the placement along the ½" (1.3 cm) seam line, ⅝" (1.6 cm) from the left-hand edge.

h. Close your zipper all of the way and place the left-hand side of the zipper onto the Front Panel top edge, **right** sides together, so the zipper tape lies ¼" (0.6 cm) below the raw edge and the bottom of the Zipper End is at the mark on the right-hand edge you just made and pin in place. Attach your zipper foot and machine baste ⅜" (1 cm) from the pinned edge.

i. Match the Lining Panel without the pocket, **right** sides together, with the Front Panel, sandwiching the zipper between them. Pin in place along the top raw edge. Sew together across the pinned edge. Unfold and press the Front and Lining Panel away from the zipper teeth.

j. Repeat Steps 9h and 9i to attach the other side of the zipper to the Back Panel and remaining Lining Panel.

k. Take one piece of cut leather and fold it in half. Thread the doubled end through the zipper pull opening, creating a

small loop, then put the two raw leather ends through the loop and pull tight to secure.

 Attach the Exterior Panels and the Lining Panels to Finish the Bag

a. Open the zipper. Pin the Front and Back Panels **right** sides together, matching the side raw edges, pushing the zipper toward the Lining Panels.

b. Pin the Lining Panels **right** sides together, matching the side raw edges and catching the top of the zipper between them.

c. Sew along the first side edge starting at the bottom of the Exterior Panels and finishing at the bottom of the Lining Panels. Repeat to sew the second side edge. Note: When sewing across the zipper, slow down or walk the needle across the metal teeth to prevent needle breakage. The bottom of the zipper should not be caught in the side seam. Clip* the curves and cut a notch at the top seam in the seam allowance. Trim excess at the top of the zipper. Press the seam allowance open.

d. Pin the Front and Back Panel bottom edge **right** sides together. Sew and press the seam allowance open. Repeat with the Lining Panels, leaving a 6" (15.2 cm) opening for turning, centered on the bottom edge.

e. On one side of the Exterior Panels align the bottom corner raw edges, **right** sides together, matching the seams, and pin. Sew and press the seam allowance toward the bottom of the bag. Repeat on the other corner of the Exterior Panels and both corners of the Lining Panels.

f. Turn the bag **right** side out by pulling the Exterior and Lining through the opening. Use a turning tool* to push out the bottom and top corners of the Exterior Panels. Press the bottom edge of the bag.

g. Fold and press ½" (1.3 cm) under on each side of the opening in the bottom of the Lining and pin in place. Slipstitch* by hand or machine stitch across the matched edges to close the opening. Push the Lining down inside the Exterior of the bag.

h. Close the zipper and your bag is complete.

Treasure Box

Finished dimensions: 8½" (21.6 cm) square at the base and 6½" (16.5 cm) tall

Inspired organization for photos, sewing notions, art supplies, and keepsakes!
Almost anyone will treasure this as a gift.

NOTES

All seams are ¼" (0.6 cm) unless otherwise stated. The seam
allowance is included in all measurements.

DESIGN INFLUENCES

Wonky Log Cabin
Triangles

TECHNIQUES USED

Patchwork
Paper Piecing
Tassel Making

MATERIALS LIST

Fabrics

From 44" (112 cm) wide light- to mid-weight fabric
⅛ yard (0.11 m) of solid for Lid Triangles
⅛ yard (0.11 m) of coordinating print for Lid Triangles
12 pieces of scrap fabrics or fat quarters that measure at least 10" x
    7" (25.4 x 17.8 cm) each for the Lid Top
⅝ yard (0.57 m) of coordinating print for the Base Bottom and
    Sides
¾ yard (0.69 m) of solid or print for Lining
⅝ yard (0.57 m) of muslin for the Quilted Panel Backing

OTHER SUPPLIES

1 package of 36" x 20" (91.4 x 50.8 cm) double-sided fusible heat
    moldable stabilizer (Bosal)
¾ yard (0.67 m) of 20" (50.8 cm) wide fusible woven interfacing
    (Pellon SF101)
36" x 45" (91.4 x 114.3 cm) piece of High-Loft Quilt Batting (Fairfield)
1 spool of all-purpose thread (Coats)
1 spool of transparent thread
1 roll of ½" (1.3 cm) double-sided tape (iCraft SuperTape)
2 skeins of pearl cotton for the Tassel Pom-poms (Coats Anchor)
2 skeins of pearl cotton in a coordinating color for the Tassel
    Strands
2 sheets of foundation paper 8½" x 11" (21.6 x 27.9 cm) (Carol
    Doak's)

ADDITIONAL TOOLS NEEDED

Heavy-duty scissors for cutting stabilizer
Large safety pins
Free-motion foot for your sewing machine
Hair dryer
Ruler that works with rotary cutter that has ¼" (0.6 cm) markings
    (CM Designs Add-A-Quarter Ruler)
1 plastic salad fork
Hand-sewing needle
Transparent tape

 Cut Out the Pattern Pieces

From the pattern sheet included with this book, cut out:
    Patchwork Template
    Triangle Template

Figure 1

Side view of Treasure Box

Figure 2

Treasure Box Patchwork on Lid Top

Cut Out the Fabric and Stabilizer Pieces

With your ruler and marking pen, mark these dimensions onto the **wrong** side of the fabric and then cut out.

From the Base Bottom and Sides Fabrics

Cut 4 – 11" x 12" (28 x 30.5 cm)
Cut 1 – 9" (22.9 cm) square for Bottom

From the Muslin

Cut 4 – 11" x 12" (28 x 30.5 cm) for the Base Sides
Cut 4 – 10¼" x 5¼" (26 x 13.3 cm) for the Lid Sides
Cut 1 – 10¼" (26 cm) square for the Lid Top

From the Batting

Cut 4 – 11" x 12" (28 x 30.5 cm) for the Base Sides
Cut 4 – 10¼" x 5¼" (26 x 13.3 cm) for the Lid Sides
Cut 1 – 10¼" (26 cm) square for the Lid Top

From the Lining Fabrics

Cut 4 – 8¾" x 7¼" (22.2 x 18.4 cm) for sides of Base
Cut 1 – 8¾" (22.2 cm) square for the Base
Cut 4 – 9" x 4" (22.9 x 10.2 cm) for sides of Lid
Cut 1 – 9" (22.9 cm) square for the Lid

From the Woven Fusible Interfacing

Cut 4 – 8¾" x 7¼" (22.2 x 18.4 cm) for sides of Base
Cut 1 – 8¾" (22.2 cm) square for the Base
Cut 4 – 9" x 4" (22.9 x 10.2 cm) for sides of Lid
Cut 1 – 9" (22.9 cm) square for the Lid

From the Heat Moldable Stabilizer

Note: Use heavy duty scissors for cutting.

Cut 2 – 16" x 6½" (40.6 x 16.5 cm) for sides of Base
Cut 1 – 8" (20.3 cm) square for the Base
Cut 2 – 16½" x 3½" (41.9 x 8.9 cm) for sides of Lid
Cut 1 – 8 ¼" (21 cm) square for the Lid

From the Triangle Template

Cut 12 from the solid
Cut 12 from the print

 Machine Quilt the Sides of the Base

a. For the first side, lay one piece of muslin in front of you and smooth out any wrinkles.

b. Place one piece of batting onto the muslin.

c. Put a Base Side, **right** side up, on top of the batting, creating a sandwich of the muslin, batting, and Base Side, then smooth out the wrinkles.

d. Use safety pins to pin the layers together every 4" (10.2 cm) to secure the layers in place.

e. Attach the free-motion foot to your machine and thread the needle with transparent thread. Free-motion quilt* around the designs on the fabric.

f. Repeat steps 3a to 3e for the other three sides. Remove your free-motion foot and replace with your standard foot.

g. Use your rotary cutter, mat, and ruler to square up* each Base Side to 9" x 7⅝" (22.9 x 19.4 cm), trimming off the excess batting, muslin, and fabric.

 Sew the Exterior Base and the Lining Base

a. Pin the short ends of two Side Base sections together and stitch with ½" (1.3 cm) seam allowance, stopping ½" (1.3 cm) from the bottom edge. Repeat with the other two Side Base sections. Then, align these two pieces with **right** sides together and sew both ends, stopping ½" (1.3 cm) from the bottom edge. Press the seams open.

b. Pin the Exterior Base Sides to the bottom edges of the Side Base pieces and stitch together with a ½" (1.3 cm) seam allowance, pivoting* at the corners.

c. Fuse the interfacing to the corresponding Lining Base pieces following the manufacturer's instructions.

d. Construct the Lining Base the same way as the Exterior Base following Steps 4a and 4b.

 Shape the Stabilizer and Complete the Base

a. On the first Side Base stabilizer piece, measure 8" (20.3 cm) from one short end and make a mark. Draw a line at this mark, perpendicular to the long edges, across the piece. Repeat on the second Side Base piece.

b. To shape the stabilizer, set your hair dryer on the highest setting. Working with one piece at a time, heat one side of the piece for about 10 seconds and then fold it along the marked line, making sure it forms a 90-degree angle. Hold the piece in place while it cools. Repeat with the second Side Base stabilizer piece.

c. Insert the stabilizer pieces into the Base, making sure the Side and Base pieces are secure in the corners and form 90-degree angles. Use the craft tape if necessary to hold the sides and bottom in place.

d. Wrap the top edge of the Exterior Base over the stabilizer to the inside of the box. Use your iron to heat set the edges of the fabric to the stabilizer. Work on a flat surface and make sure your iron does not touch the stabilizer.

e. Slip the Lining Base into the box. Push the bottom and side seams into the corner edges and along the Base seams.

f. Fold the top edge of the Lining down to the **wrong** side, toward the stabilizer, so that it is slightly below the edge of the Exterior Base. Sandwich the craft tape between the Lining and the Exterior Base along the top edge, then remove the backing from the tape. Press firmly to adhere the Lining to the stabilizer. Set the Base aside while you construct the Lid.

 Sew the Triangles Together for the Lid Sides

a. Take four of the solid Triangles and cut them in half, from the top point to the bottom center.

b. Sew three print Triangles to two solid Triangles using Figure 1 as a guide.

c. Take two of the half Triangles and sew them to the ends of the print Triangles. You should have a piece that measures 9¼" x 3¾" (23.5 x 9.5 cm).

d. Repeat with the rest of the Triangle pieces to make the other three Lid Sides.

e. To quilt the Lid Sides, lay one muslin piece on a flat surface and smooth out any wrinkles.

f. Place one piece of batting on the muslin.

g. Center one Lid Side, **right** side up, on top of the batting, creating a sandwich of the muslin, batting, and Lid Side. The muslin and batting will be larger.

h. Use safety pins and pin the layers together every 4" (10.2 cm) to secure.

i. Thread the machine's needle with transparent thread and stitch-in-the-ditch* along all of the seams.

j. Trim the muslin and batting down to the same size as the Lid Side.

k. Repeat with all of the Lid Side pieces.

 Paper Piece the Box Lid

a. Tape the two sheets of foundation paper together, overlapping ½" (1.3 cm), using the transparent tape.

b. Trace the Patchwork Template onto the foundation paper, making sure your lines are straight, as you will be following these lines when you are stitching. Add a 1" (2.5 cm) seam allowance to all outside edges. Transfer the numbers of each section onto the tracing. Note: The Patchwork Template is a mirror image of the completed Box Lid.

c. Using Figure 2 as a guide, decide on the placement of the twelve fabrics in the patchwork and put them in order from 1 to 12.

d. Place the piece for the patchwork's center (Section 1) on the **wrong** side of the paper template. Then, place the fabric for Section 2 **right** sides together with the Section 1 piece. Make sure that both fabrics extend ¼" (0.6 cm) past Sections 1 and 2 on the template. With the paper on top, pin through both fabrics and the paper.

e. Shorten your stitch length to 1.5 and stitch along the line between Sections 1 and 2.

f. Fold back the paper along the line and use a ruler with ¼" (0.6 cm) markings to help trim the seam to ¼" (0.6 cm).

g. Turn the foundation so the fabric is up and open the fabric so it lies flat. Press the seams toward Section 2.

h. Turn the foundation paper-side up and check that the fabric covers Section 2 by at least ¼" (0.6 cm) around all edges.

i. Place the fabric for Section 3 **right** sides together against the Sections 1 and 2 fabrics. Make sure that all fabrics extend at least ¼" (0.6 cm) past the drawn lines for their section. Sew along the line between Sections 1, 2, and 3.

j. Continue to sew the sections around the center piece in numerical order, trimming and pressing as you go.

k. When you finish with Section 12, cut out the patchwork block along the outside line of the template and remove the paper backing.

 Machine Quilt the Box Lid

a. To quilt the Lid Top, lay the muslin piece in front of you and smooth out any wrinkles.

b. Place the piece of batting on the muslin.

c. Center the Lid Top **right** side up on top of the batting, creating a sandwich of the muslin, batting, and top. The muslin and batting will be larger.

d. Use safety pins and pin the layers together every 4" (10.2 cm) to secure.

e. Thread the machine's needle with transparent thread and stitch-in-the-ditch* along all of the seams.

f. Use your rotary cutter, mat, and ruler to trim off the excess batting, muslin, and fabric so the Lid Top measures 8¾" (22.2 cm) square.

 Sew the Exterior and Lining Lids

a. Pin the short ends of two Lid Side sections **right** sides together and stitch together, stopping ¼" (0.6 cm) from the top edges. Repeat with the other two Lid Side sections. Then bring both sewn sections **right** sides together and sew both ends, stopping ¼" (0.6 cm) from the top edges. Press the seams open.

b. Pin the Lid Top edges to the four top edges of the Sides and stitch together, pivoting at the corners.

c. Fuse the interfacing to the corresponding Lining Lid Side pieces following the manufacturer's instructions.

d. Construct the Lining Lid the same as the Exterior following Steps 9a and 9b.

Make the Tassels

a. Wrap the pearl cotton 40 times around the salad fork tines. Take a 5" (12.7 cm) length and tie all of the wraps together tightly with a knot, sliding off the fork for a tighter knot. Don't trim off the ends of the knot. Cut the untied end of the wraps and fluff. Make 12 pom-poms.

b. Cut three 5" (12.7 cm) strands of the coordinating pearl cotton for the strands and tie them in a knot at one end. Braid the strands together, then knot the bottom, clipping the threads close. Make 12.

c. Now tie the long tails from each pom-pom to the bottom of each braid and tie a knot. Trim the threads. Do this for all 12.

d. Bring three braids together at the top, making one strand longer than the other two. Knot together about 2¼" (5.7 cm) up. Repeat with all of the Tassels.

e. Hand sew a Tassel Set to each inside corner of the Lid, placing the knot so that it will be covered by the Lining.

Shape the Stabilizer and Complete the Lid Lining

a. On the first Lid Lining Side stabilizer piece measure in 8¼" (21 cm) from one short end and make a mark. Draw a line perpendicular to this mark across the piece. Repeat on the second Lid Lining Side piece.

b. Use the same method in Steps 5b and 5c to complete the Lid Lining.

c. Fold down the bottom edge of the Lining toward the stabilizer, so that it is slightly below the Exterior Lid edge. Sandwich the craft tape between the Lining and the Exterior Lid along the bottom edge; remove the backing from the tape. Press the inside of the Lid to adhere the Lining to the Stabilizer.

Talisman Necklace

Finished length: 17" (43.2 cm) • Talisman size: 1½" (3.8 cm) tall x 1¼" (3.2 cm) base

The Talisman Necklace is an easy style add-on with charm and elegance.
Delicate beading and hand-stitched details make this a one-of-a-kind treasure!

NOTES

All seams are ⅛" (0.3 cm) unless otherwise stated. The seam
allowance is included in all measurements.

DESIGN INFLUENCE

Triangles

TECHNIQUES USED

Patchwork
Beadwork

Figure 1

— Silk Sari Ribbon

— Talisman Charm

MATERIALS LIST

Fabrics

Use Figure 1 as a guide
From 44" (112 cm) wide light- to mid-weight fabric
⅛ yard (0.11 m) each of 9 different prints and solids for the
    Talisman Charms

OTHER SUPPLIES

½ yard (0.5 m) of 20" (50.8 cm) wide fusible woven interfacing
    (Pellon SF101)

Two 1-yard (0.92-m) lengths of silk sari ribbon strips (Leilani Arts)
    or other lightweight fabric cut into 1" x 36" (2.5 x 91.4 cm) strips
1 skein each of 3 coordinating colors of embroidery floss (Coats)
1 spool of coordinating all-purpose thread (Coats)
1 spool of transparent thread (Coats)
3 coordinating colors of seed beads (about 100 of each bead color)
Approximately 50 fringe 3.44 mm teardrop seed beads (Miyuki
    Bead)
7 bead caps with holes at the top and around the edges (7 mm)
    (Antique Brass Filigree Bead Caps – MKBeads)

ADDITIONAL TOOLS NEEDED

Chalk pencil or fabric marker
Turning tool
21 cotton balls
Hemostat (found at most drugstores)
1 hand sewing needle
1 hand-embroidery needle (Prym-Dritz)
1 beading needle
Fabric glue (Alenes)
Needle-nose pliers

 Cut Out the Talisman Charm Templates

From the pattern sheet included with this book, cut out:
Talisman Charm Side
Talisman Charm Base

 Cut Out the Fabric Pieces

From the Fusible Woven Interfacing
Cut 9 pieces – 4" x 9" (10.2 x 22.9 cm)

From Each of the 9 Fabrics

Cut 1 piece – 4" x 9" (10.2 x 22.9 cm)

a. Fuse one interfacing* piece to the **wrong** side of each of
the nine fabrics. With your fabric marking pen, number the
pieces from 1 to 9 on the interfacing side.

b. Each Charm is made of three sides and one base. Using the
marking pen, trace the templates* onto the interfacing side
of the fabric pieces and cut all the pieces. Then, arrange

the pieces into seven stacks, following the table for each of the Charms.

TABLE 1

Charm	Side Fabrics	Base Fabric
One	1, 2, 3	4
Two	4, 5, 6	9
Three	7, 4, 1	6
Four	3, 8, 6	5
Five	4, 9, 3	7
Six	4, 1, 6	8
Seven	2, 3, 7	1

 Make the Charms

a. For the first Charm, start by sewing two of the Sides together from the widest part to the narrow top point.

b. Next, sew the Base to the bottom of the two Sides.

c. Sew the third Side to the Base and the two Sides, but leave a 1" (2.5 cm) opening.

d. Trim* off the excess seam allowance at the points, being careful not to clip the stitching.

e. Turn the Charm **right** side out and push out the points using a turning tool.

f. Stuff the Charm with two or three cotton balls. I found that using a hemostat for stuffing made it very easy.

g. Thread the hand-sewing needle with a double thread and tie a knot. Hide the knot on the inside of the Charm and then slipstitch* the opening closed, pulling the remaining thread up through the top point and tying off.

h. Repeat with the remaining Charms.

 Embellish the Charms

Note: As you work, hide the knots at the top point of the Charm, entering and exiting through this end, being careful not to pull too hard to pucker it.

a. Start with the first Charm and one color of floss. Thread three strands of floss into a hand-embroidery needle and make a knot at the end.

b. Sew along each side seam of the Charm using a whipstitch*, spacing your stitches ⅛ to ³⁄₁₆" (0.3 to 0.5 cm) apart. Pull the floss up through the top point and tie a knot, leaving a 6" to 8" (15.2 to 20.3 cm) tail.

c. Repeat for the remaining Charms, switching the embroidery floss colors to your liking.

d. For all of the bead stitching, thread your beading needle with a double strand of transparent thread and tie a knot at the end. Tip: Kink the thread with a pair of needle-nose pliers

where you want the knot to go. When you tie the knot at this kink, it will be less likely to shift. Use the pliers to help pull the knot tight.

e. Hand stitch the seed beads along the side seams, placing the beads over the whipstitches. Vary the color of the beads for each of the Charms. (See Figure 2.)

Figure 2

Bead Cap

Charm tied to silk ribbon with embroidery floss

Seed beads stitched along seams

Whipstitch with embroidery floss along seams

f. Choose four of the Charms to sew the teardrop beads to. These beads will only get sewn to one side. Hand stitch nine or ten beads per Charm. (See Figure 3.)

g. Thread the embroidery floss tail up through the hole in the top of a bead cap. Then hand stitch it to the top of each Charm along the bottom edge of the cap, using transparent thread.

Figure 3

Teardrop beads sewn to Charm side

 Finish the Necklace

a. Bring all the ends of both silk sari ribbons together and tie a knot.

b. Lay the ribbon down on a flat surface and arrange the Charms around the ribbon, remembering the knot will sit at the nape of your neck.

c. To secure each Charm to the ribbon, wrap the embroidery floss tail around the ribbon, making sure the Charm is pulled close, and then tie the floss to itself in a secure knot above the bead cap. Trim the floss tail and apply a small dot of fabric glue to the knot.

Dressing Room

Bohemian Fashion Statements

As you dress up your wardrobe, special handwork touches and unique construction details personalize every piece.

Divine Patchwork Dress

Finished sizes: XS – XXXL

Finished length (from back neck to hem): XS – L: 39" (99.1 cm) • XL – XXXL: 40" (101.6 cm)

Colorful patchwork details mix with bold prints in this modern silhouette.
Easy to wear and looks gorgeous dressed up or down!

NOTES

All seams are ½" (1.3 cm) unless otherwise stated. The seam allowance is included in all pattern pieces.

DESIGN INFLUENCE

Triangles

TECHNIQUE USED

Patchwork

MATERIALS LIST

Fabrics

From 44" (112 cm) wide light- to mid-weight fabric

For sizes XS – L:

¼ yard (0.23 m) each of 6 coordinating prints and solids for Patchwork Triangles

½ yard (0.46 m) of coordinating print for Back Bodice

1 yard (0.92 m) of solid for Bodice Lining

1¾ yards (1.6 m) of coordinating print for Skirt

2 pieces, 20" x 3" (50.8 x 7.6 cm), of coordinating print or ribbon for Neckline Band

⅝ yard (0.58 m) of muslin for Front Bodice Patchwork Backing

For sizes XL – XXXL:

⅜ yard (0.34 m) each of 6 coordinating prints and solids for Patchwork Triangles

⅝ yard (0.58 m) of coordinating print for Back Bodice

1¼ yards (1.14 m) of solid for Bodice Lining

1¾ yards (1.6 m) of coordinating print for Skirt

2 pieces, 20" x 3" (50.8 x 7.6 cm), of coordinating fabric or ribbon for Neckline Band

⅝ yard (0.58 m) of muslin for Front Bodice Patchwork Backing

OTHER SUPPLIES

1 spool of coordinating all-purpose thread (Coats)

1 spool of metallic thread (Coats)

⅛ yard (0.11 m) of 20" (50.8 cm) wide fusible knit interfacing (Pellon EK130)

Temporary spray adhesive for fabric (505 Spray and Fix)

Sewer's Aid thread lubricant (Dritz)

ADDITIONAL TOOLS NEEDED

Masking tape and marker

Universal needle for fine fabrics 70/10

Metallic needle 80/12

CHART 1
BODY MEASUREMENTS

Women's Sizes	Bust	Waist	Hips
X-Small (2–4)	32½" (85.1 cm)	26" (66 cm)	36" (91.4 cm)
Small (6–8)	34½" (87.6 cm)	28" (71.1 cm)	38" (96.5 cm)
Medium (10–12)	36" (91.4 cm)	30½" (77.5 cm)	40½" (102.9 cm)
Large (14–16)	39" (99.1 cm)	33½" (85.1 cm)	43½" (110.5 cm)
X-Large (18)	42" (106.7 cm)	37½" (95.3 cm)	47½" (120.7 cm)
XX-Large (20)	45" (114.3 cm)	39" (99.1 cm)	50" (127 cm)
XXX-Large (22)	48" (121.9 cm)	41" (104.1 cm)	54" (137.2 cm)

 Cut Out the Pattern Pieces

a. Using your tape measure, measure your Bust (around the fullest part), your Waist, and Hip (around the fullest part across the top of your upper thigh). Then follow the chart to determine the size for your Dress. If your measurements differ from those listed, adjust the pattern pieces before placing them on your fabric. Adjustments can be made to the bodice pattern piece by adding or subtracting from the appropriate lines, and drawing a new cutting line. Choose the size that matches your bust and waist measurements and connect the corresponding lines with a smooth, even line.

b. Cut out the pattern pieces and template.

From the pattern sheet included with this book, cut out

Bodice Front

Bodice Back

Neckline Band

Triangle Template

Cut Out All the Pieces from the Fabric

a. Cut the Bodice pieces.

From Back Bodice Fabric

Cut 1 Back Bodice on fold*

From Lining Fabric

Cut 1 Back Bodice on fold
(Front Bodice Lining will be cut in Step 5.)

Figure 1

Skirt Measurement Layout Front / Back

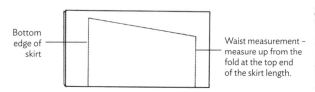

Length of skirt – measure along folded edge.

b. Cut the Skirt Back.

From the Skirt Fabric:

Cut 1 Skirt Back using the following instructions:
Refer to Figure 1. Fold your fabric in half lengthwise, matching the selvage edges. Using a ruler and marking pen, measure and mark directly on your fabric these measurements for your size.

1. For Skirt Length measure along folded edge:
   27" (68.6 cm) for XS – L
   28" (71.1 cm) for XL – XXXL
2. For the Waist, measure up from the fold at the top end of the Skirt Length:
   XS: 12" (30.5 cm)
   S: 12¼" (31.1 cm)
   M: 12¾" (32.3 cm)
   L: 13½" (34.3 cm)
   XL: 14¼" (36.2 cm)
   XXL: 15" (38.1 cm)
   XXL: 15⅞" (40.3 cm)
3. For the Hem width, measure up from the fold at the bottom end of the Skirt Length:
   XS: 16" (40.6 cm)
   S: 16¼" (41.3 cm)
   M: 16¾" (42.6 cm)
   L: 17½" (44.5 cm)
   XL: 18¼" (45.6 cm)
   XXL: 19" (48.3 cm)
   XXXL: 20" (50.8 cm)

Connect the ends of the Waist and Hem lines with a straight line to make the side edges; cut along the drawn lines.

c. Cut the Skirt Front.

From the Skirt Fabric

Cut 1 Skirt Back using the following instructions:
Refer to Figure 1. Fold your fabric in half lengthwise, matching the selvage edges. Using a ruler and marking pen, measure and mark directly on your fabric these measurements for your size.

1. For Skirt Length measure along folded edge:
   27" (68.6 cm) for XS – L
   28" (71.1 cm) for XL – XXXL
2. For the Waist, measure up from the fold at the top end of the Skirt Length:
   XS: 12¼" (31.1 cm)
   S: 12⅜" (31.4 cm)
   M: 12¾" (32.4 cm)
   L: 13½" (34.3 cm)
   XL: 14¼" (36.2 cm)
   XXL: 15" (38.1 cm)
   XXXL: 15¾" (40 cm)
3. For the Hem width, measure up from the fold at the bottom end of the Skirt Length:
   XS: 16" (40.6 cm)
   S: 16¼" (41.3 cm)
   M: 16¾" (42.6 cm)
   L: 17½" (44.5 cm)
   XL: 18¼" (46.4 cm)
   XXL: 19" (48.3 cm)
   XXXL: 20" (50.8 cm)

Connect the ends of the Waist and Hem lines with a straight line to make the side edges; cut along the drawn lines.

d. Cut the muslin.

Cut 2 panels:

   XS – L: 22" x 18" (55.9 x 45.7 cm)
   XL – XXXL: 22" x 22½" (55.9 x 57.2 cm)

e. Cut the Neckline Band pieces.
Fussy cut* two mirror image pieces using the pattern piece (be sure to flip the pattern piece over so you cut a left and right front.)

f. Cut the Patchwork Fabrics.
Figure 2 shows the layout of the Patchwork Triangles on the Front

Bodice. Use this illustration as a guide for the placement of your fabric prints. You may find it helpful to mark each print A to F using a marker and masking tape on the **wrong** side of each strip as it is cut.

Use your rotary cutter, mat, and ruler to cut strips from each of the six Patchwork Fabrics.

For sizes XS – L:
Cut 2 strips of each fabric: 3" (7.6 cm) x the width of fabric* (wof)

For sizes XL – XXXL:
Cut 2 strips of each fabric: 3" (7.6 cm) x wof

Then, on each strip, use the Triangle Template and a chalk pencil to trace the following number of triangles onto the **right** side of the fabric, flipping the template to alternate the direction of the triangles as you work across the strip. Use Table 1 to find the number of triangles needed from each fabric for your size.

TABLE 1
TRIANGLE PATCHWORK

	XS – L	XL – XXL	XXXL
Fabric A	30	40	40
Fabric B	30	36	36
Fabric C	22	28	28
Fabric D	22	24	26
Fabric E	18	24	24
Fabric F	18	22	24

Figure 2

Patchwork Bodice

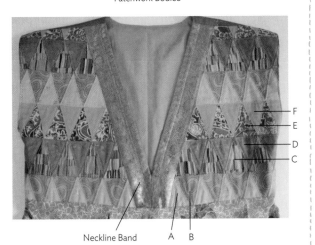

Neckline Band   A   B

Transfer the Dots and Pleat Lines

a. Use your chalk pencil to transfer the dots* to the **wrong** side of the Bodice Back Panels, Back Lining Panels, and Neckline Band.

b. Cut two 1" (2.5 cm) squares from the fusible knit interfacing. Fuse a square over the Neckline Dot on the **wrong** side of the Neckline Band pieces. Redraw the dot.

c. For the Pleats on both the Front and Back Skirt, working along the waistline, measure the three lengths given from the center fold and mark each on both sides of the center fold, for a total of six marks at the waist line each on the Skirt Front and Back.

XS/S: 1", 4", 6" (2.5 cm, 10.2 cm, 15.2 cm)
M: 1", 4½", 6½" (2.5 cm, 11.4 cm, 16.5 cm)
L: 1", 5", 7" (2.5 cm, 12.7 cm, 17.8 cm)
XL: 1", 5¾", 7¾" (2.5 cm, 14.6 cm, 19.7 cm)
XXL: 1", 6½", 8½" (2.5 cm, 16.5 cm, 21.6 cm)
XXXL: 1", 7", 9" (2.5 cm, 17.8 cm, 22.9 cm)

Make the Patchwork for the Front Bodice Panels

Note: The Front Bodice Panels will be constructed as mirror images of each other. Each row of triangles will begin at the neckline with a triangle pointing up, and alternate between upward and downward pointing triangles. The triangles shape the angle at the Neckline Band. Refer to Figure 2 when laying out the rows.

a. Lay out the triangles in rows for each side of the Front Bodice. The numbers in Table 2 for each row refer to each side of the Front Bodice. The first number corresponds to the first fabric listed and is always the triangle closest to the neckline.

TABLE 2
FRONT BODICE

Row	Fabric	Size Range		
		XS – L	XL – XXL	XXXL
1	A/B	6/6 each side	9/8 each side	9/8 each side
2	C/D	6/6	8/7	8/8
3	E/F	5/5	7/6	7/6
4	A/B	5/5	6/6	6/6
5	C/D	5/5	6/5	6/5
6	E/F	4/4	5/5	5/5
7	A/B	4/4	5/4	5/4

b. Starting with Row 1 on the first Front Bodice, sew Triangles A and B with **right** sides together, starting with an A Triangle, pointing up, and working from the neckline edge toward the side seam, using a ¼" (0.6 cm) seam. Press all the seam allowances open.

c. Sew Row 2 using the C and D Triangles, working in the same direction as Row 1 and starting with a C Triangle. Press all the seam allowances open.

d. Continue to sew and press the triangles for all the remaining rows in the same manner.

e. Repeat Steps 4b to 4d to complete the second side of the Front Bodice, starting with the same triangle letter for each row, but working in the opposite direction.

f. On the First Front Bodice, pin Rows 1 and 2 **right** sides together, matching the triangle points and seam lines. The triangles that are closest to the neckline will form the angled neckline. Sew along the pinned edge using a ¼" (0.6 cm) seam. Press open.

g. Continue pinning and sewing the rows, in order, pressing each seam open as you go and maintaining the angle for the Neckline Band. (See Figure 3.)

Figure 3

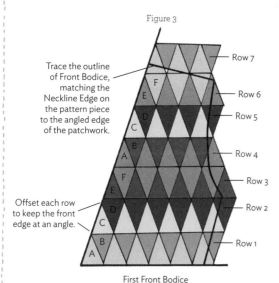

Trace the outline of Front Bodice, matching the Neckline Edge on the pattern piece to the angled edge of the patchwork.

Offset each row to keep the front edge at an angle.

Row 7
Row 6
Row 5
Row 4
Row 3
Row 2
Row 1

First Front Bodice

h. Repeat Steps 4f and 4g for the second Front Bodice, making sure the neckline angle goes in the opposite direction, so the two bodices mirror each other.

Construct the Front Bodice

a. Lay the two patchwork panels in front of you with the **right** sides facing up.

b. Place the Front Bodice pattern piece onto the first patchwork

panel, lining up the neckline edge on the pattern with the angled edge on the patchwork. Pin the pattern to the fabric. Cut out the first Front Bodice. Repeat with the second patchwork panel by flipping the pattern piece over to cut the mirror image of the Bodice.

c. Match the first Neckline Band with the corresponding Bodice Panel. Pin the Band to the Panel **right** sides together along the neckline edge. Stitch a ¼" (0.6 cm) seam along this pinned edge and then press the seam open. Repeat with the second Neckline Band and patchwork panel.

d. Use the joined Front Bodice/Neckline Band pieces as the pattern pieces to cut two Lining Bodice pieces from the lining fabric and set aside.

e. Lay the two pieces of muslin out in front of you on a flat surface. Spray lightly with temporary spray adhesive.

f. Place one Front Bodice **right** side up on each piece of muslin and smooth out any wrinkles; the Front Bodice should adhere to the muslin.

g. Use a metallic needle in your machine. Thread your needle with metallic thread and lower your tension setting. Tip: Use a thread lubricant such as Sewer's Aid to keep your thread running smoothly through your machine.

h. Working from the middle of each panel out, topstitch* inside each triangle ⅛" (0.3 cm) from all seams.

i. Change your needle and needle thread back, and machine baste* ½" (1.3 cm) around the outside edges of the Front Bodices. Carefully trim away the excess muslin. Press each Front Bodice gently using a press cloth.

Sew the Exterior and Lining Bodices Together at the Neckline Edge

a. Hold the two Front Bodice pieces with **right** sides together, matching at the Neckline Dot. Starting at the dot, sew along the pinned edges, joining the neckline.

b. With **right** sides together, match the shoulder seams of the Front and Back Bodices and pin. Stitch along the pinned edges and then press the seam allowances open.

c. Stay stitch* slightly less than ½" (1.3 cm) along the front and back necklines, pivoting* at the center front seam.

d. Repeat Steps 5a to 5c with the Front and Back Lining pieces.

e. Pin the Exterior and the Lining Bodices around the neckline, matching the shoulder seams and the center front dot. Sew together, pivoting at the dot. Clip* the seam allowances along the curved part of the neckline, then again at the Neckline Dot, being careful not to clip the stitches. Trim the seam allowances* to ¼" (0.6 cm) and then press open.

f. Press the neckline seam allowance toward the lining. Under stitch* ⅛" (0.3 cm) away from the seam on the **right** side of the lining. Turn the lining to the inside and press flat along the neckline edge.

 Sew the Exterior and Lining Bodices Together at the Armhole

a. Stay stitch ½" (1.3 cm) along the edges of the Exterior and Lining armholes.

b. Match the side seams of the Front and Back Bodices and pin **right** sides together. Stitch along the pinned edges and then press the seam allowances open. Repeat for the Lining side seams.

c. Bring the Bodices **wrong** sides together, matching the side seams and the shoulder seams.

d. Fold and press under the ½" (1.3 cm) seam allowances along the stay stitching lines around both armholes so they are tucked in between the Bodice and Lining. Align the folded edges of each armhole and pin both edges together.

e. Edge stitch* the pinned edges around each armhole.

f. Pin the bottom edges of the Exterior and Lining Bodices together. Machine baste ½" (1.3 cm) to hold together while you attach the Skirt.

 Make the Pleats and Sew the Skirt

a. There are three pleats on both the Front and Back Skirts. To make the first pleat, fold the skirt **right** sides together, matching two marked dots, and pin. Press a crease on the fold. Sew a 1" (2.5 cm) long seam, starting at the waistline and stitching down, backstitching* at the end. Then, align this seam with the crease and press the pleat flat.

b. Repeat for the remaining pleats on both skirts.

c. Pin the Front and Back Skirts together at the sides with **right** sides together. Stitch, then press the seams open. Finish the raw edges using an overcast stitch*.

 Attach the Skirt to the Bodice

Pin the Skirt to the Bodice, **right** sides together, matching side seams, center front and center back. Stitch together and press the seam allowance toward the Bodice. Finish the seam with an overcast stitch.

 Hem the Dress

a. Fold the bottom edge of the skirt ½" (1.3 cm) toward the **wrong** side and press.

b. Fold this edge over again, enclosing the raw edges, and press. Edge stitch along the upper folded edge.

Bohemian Wrap

Finished sizes: Two sizes: S – L & XL – XXXL

Finished Dimensions: S – L: 33" (83.8 cm) length from back neck to hem, 35" (88.9 cm) front length, 19" (48.3 cm) sleeve length
XL – XXXL: 33" (83.8 cm) length from back neck to hem, 37" (94 cm) front length, 19" (48.3 cm) sleeve length

Add easy elegance to any outfit with this luxurious silk wrap made with vintage sari fabric.

NOTES

All seams are ¼" (0.6 cm) unless otherwise stated. The seam allowance is included in all measurements.

DESIGN INFLUENCE

Log Cabin

TECHNIQUE USED

Patchwork

Figure 1

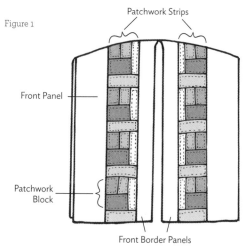

Patchwork Strips

Front Panel

Patchwork Block

Front Border Panels

MATERIALS LIST

Notes: For the body of this wrap I used a recycled silk sari that measured 5 yards (4.5 m) long and 45" (114 cm) wide. I did not use the entire thing, but instead "fussy cut"* my pieces from the yardage, using only about half of the full piece, reserving the rest for another project. For the patchwork on the wrap I used scraps from three coordinating saris that I had from other projects. Lightweight silks, polyesters, and rayons can be used in place of the sari fabric. Please allow extra yardage for fussy cutting your pieces. The equivalent yardage is listed following.

Every wrap will differ depending on your sari or fabric print and where you take your pieces from it. If you are using a sari for your scarf, Figure 2 gives you a general idea of the basic parts of a sari when it

is laid open. You will notice that there are several distinct areas you can use to design your scarf's unique look. For example, I positioned my front border panels along the wide sari borders. This gave me a beautiful decorative and finished edge along the front of my wrap. Because every sari has its own individual characteristics, take time to determine which sections you wish to use for the different parts of your wrap.

Figure 2

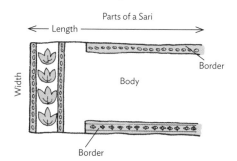

Parts of a Sari

Length

Width

Body

Border

Border

Fabrics

Use Figures 1 and 2 as guides for sari selection and placement

From 45" (114 cm) wide lightweight sari or other lightweight silky fabric

3¼ yards (3 m) of main sari fabric for the Front Panels, Back Panel, and Front Border Panels (for both sizes)

⅜ yard (0.34 m) of coordinating sari fabric for Patchwork A, D, and E

¼ yard (0.23 m) of coordinating sari fabric for Patchwork B

¼ yard (0.23 m) of coordinating sari fabric for Patchwork C

OTHER SUPPLIES

1 spool of coordinating all-purpose thread (Coats)

Temporary fabric spray adhesive (505 Spray & Fix Temporary Fabric Adhesive)

Heavy spray starch

ADDITIONAL TOOLS NEEDED

Ruler and pencil

1 sheet of tracing paper, 9" x 12" (22.7 x 30.5 cm), and pencil

Universal needle for fine fabrics 70/10

Fine silk straight pins (Prym Dritz)

Narrow hem foot for your sewing machine (optional)

CHART 1
BODY MEASUREMENTS

Women's Sizes	Bust	Waist	Hips
Small (6–8)	34½" (87.6 cm)	28" (71.1 cm)	38" (96.5 cm)
Medium (10–12)	36" (91.4 cm)	30½" (77.5 cm)	40½" (102.9 cm)
Large (14–16)	39" (99.1 cm)	33½" (85.1 cm)	43½" (110.5 cm)
X-Large (18)	42" (106.7 cm)	37½" (95.3 cm)	47½" (120.7 cm)
XX-Large (20)	45" (114.3 cm)	39" (99.1 cm)	50" (127 cm)
XXX-Large (22)	48" (121.9 cm)	41" (104.1 cm)	54" (137.2 cm)

 Measure and Cut the Pattern Pieces

Using a ruler and pencil, measure and mark the dimensions
following onto the sheet of tracing paper. Then cut along the
marked lines.

Patchwork Piece A: 4¼" x 2" (10.8 x 5.1 cm)

Patchwork Piece B: 4¼" x 3" (10.8 x 7.6 cm)

Patchwork Piece C: 3⅛" x 4½" (7.9 x 11.4 cm)

Patchwork Piece D: 6⅞" x 1½" (17.5 x 3.8 cm)

Patchwork Piece E: 2⅝" x 5½" (6.7 x 14 cm)

 Measure and Cut the Fabric

Note: To help reduce the slipperiness of lightweight silky fabrics,
lightly spray with heavy starch to give the fabric some body
and make working with it easier. Test on a small section of the
fabric first, following the manufacturer's instructions.

a. Cut the Front, Back, and Front Border pieces.

Lay the main fabric flat. Using a ruler and chalk pencil or marking
pen, measure and mark the dimensions for the Front, Back, and
Front Border Panels directly onto the fabric.

For sizes S – L

Cut 1 Back Panel: 40" (101.6 cm) wide x 33⅝" (85.4 cm) long

Cut 2 Front Panels: 13⅝" (34.6 cm) wide x 35⅜" (85.4 cm) long

Cut 2 Front Border Panels: 6⅝" (16.8 cm) wide x 35⅜"
(85.4 cm) long

For sizes XL – XXXL

Cut 1 Back Panel: 40" (101.6 cm) wide x 33⅝" (85.4 cm) long

Cut 2 Front Panels: 13⅝" (34.6 cm) wide x 37⅜" (94.9 cm) long

Cut 2 Front Border Panels: 5⅝" (14.3 cm) wide x 37⅜"
(94.9 cm) long

b. Angle the shoulder seam on the Back Panel.

To make the angle for the shoulder seam on the Back Panel, fold
the panel in half widthwise, matching the short edges, and

press lightly along the folded edge. Measure ⅝" (1.6 cm) (S –
L) or ¾" (1.9 cm) (XL – XXXL) in from the fold along the top
edge and make a mark. Next, measure down 2¾" (7 cm) from
the top along the outside (cut) edge and make a mark. Use
your ruler and chalk pencil or marking pen to connect these
two marks with a straight line. Pin to hold the fabric together
and cut along this drawn line. (See Figure 3.) Set the Back
Panel aside for now.

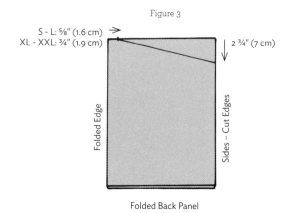

Figure 3

Folded Back Panel

c. Cut the Patchwork Panel pieces.

Using the paper pattern pieces you made in Step 1 and the three
coordinating fabrics:

Cut 8 each of Patchwork Pieces A, D, and E from the first coordinating fabric (for sizes XL – XXXL only, cut an additional two
Patchwork Piece E's, a total of 10).

Cut 8 of Patchwork Piece B from the second coordinating fabric.

Cut 8 of Patchwork Piece C from the third coordinating fabric.

 Sew the Front Border Panels to the Front Panels

Note: If you used the finished border edge of the sari for the
Front Border when cutting out your pieces, skip Step 3a.

a. Finish the long front edge of the first Front Border Panel with
a narrow hem. Make the narrow hem by first stitching a ⅜"
(1 cm) seam along the edge, then pressing this edge toward
the **wrong** side along the stitching line. Then fold under the
raw edge to meet the stitching line, and pin in place. Spray
lightly with spray starch and press. Stitch a narrow hem close
to the folded edge and press again. Repeat with the second
Front Border Panel.

b. Pin the unfinished edge of a Front Border Panel to a Front
Panel, **wrong** sides together, and pin in place. Stitch together.
Do not press the seam allowance yet. Repeat with the second
Front Border Panel and Front Panel. Set the sewn Front Panels

aside while you construct the patchwork. Note: The seam allowances will be covered later with the patchwork.

 Sew the Patchwork Blocks

Note: You will make two strip sets of Patchwork Blocks that mirror each other, one set for the left side of the wrap and one set for the right. Only the placement of Patchwork Piece D differs. Follow Figure 4 for the order of construction for both sets. The image shown is for the left side.

a. With **right** sides together, sew Patchwork Pieces A and B together; press the seam toward A.

b. Sew Patchwork Piece C to the bottom of the A/B block. Press the seam toward C.

c. Sew Patchwork Piece D to the B/C piece. Press the seam toward D.

d. Sew E to the bottom of the block. Press the seam toward E.

e. Repeat Steps 4a to 4d three more times for the left-hand side Patchwork Blocks. Put these blocks in a pile.

f. Repeat Steps 4a to 4d for the remaining four blocks, but sew Patchwork Piece D next to A/C rather than B/C. Put these blocks in a separate pile for the right-hand side.

g. Sew the four left-hand side Patchwork Blocks together. Align the bottom edge of one of the Patchwork Blocks with the top edge of the next block, **right** sides together, pin, and stitch the seam together. Continue with the remaining left-hand block pieces, to make a long strip. Note: For the XL – XXL, sew the extra E piece to the top of each strip. Press the seams toward the top of the strip. Then repeat with the right-hand Patchwork Block pieces.

h. Stitch ¼" (0.6 cm) from the long, raw edge of one Patchwork Strip closest to the side of the Wrap (the side with the A/C/E pieces). Repeat with the second strip.

 Sew the Patchwork to the Wrap

a. Pin the non-stitched side of one Patchwork Strip, **right** sides together, to the corresponding Front Border Panel along the seam where you attached the Front Panel, matching the raw edges. Stitch all three layers together over the previous stitching. Press the seam toward the Front Panel. Repeat with the second Patchwork Strip and Front Border Panel/Front Panel.

b. Lightly spray the **wrong** side of the Patchwork Strip with temporary fabric adhesive spray and then position it so that the **wrong** side is against the **right** side of the Front Panel, encasing the seam allowances. Smooth out any wrinkles. Fold under the ¼" (0.6 cm) along the stitched edge and pin the patchwork to the Front Panel along this fold. Edge stitch*

along this pinned edge and press. Repeat with the second Patchwork Strip and Front Panel.

c. Edge stitch through all layers inside each Patchwork Piece, ⅛" (0.3 cm) from each seam. See Figure 4 for stitching.

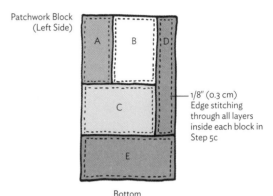

Figure 4

Patchwork Block (Left Side)

⅛" (0.3 cm) Edge stitching through all layers inside each block in Step 5c

Bottom

Construct the Wrap

a. Angle the shoulder seam on the Front Panel. The shoulder seams on the Front Panels need to be cut at an angle to match the Back Panel. On the first Front Panel measure 2¾" (7 cm) down from the top along the outside edge (the side without the Border) and make a mark. Use your ruler and chalk pencil or marking pen and connect the top front edge with this new mark. Cut along this drawn line. Repeat on the second Front Panel, making sure that the panels mirror each other. Note: You will be cutting through part of the Patchwork Strip.

b. Note: Use pins or temporary adhesive spray in the shoulder area if necessary to hold the patchwork in place while you sew the shoulder seams. Pin the Front and Back Panels together at the shoulder seams with the **wrong** sides together, leaving a 1¼" (3.2 cm) gap at the top of the Back Panel between the two marks you made in Step 2b. Stitch across the pinned edges with a ¼" (0.6 cm) seam allowance. Press the seam open. Next, turn the seam so the **right** sides are together and pin in place. Sew together using a ⅜" (1 cm) seam allowance; press the seam allowances toward the Back.

c. Stay stitch* the back neck edge with a ⅜" (1 cm) seam between the shoulder seams. Sew a narrow hem in this area to finish the back neck edge.

d. Following the narrow hem instructions in Step 3a, create a narrow hem along any unfinished edges.

Embellished Infinity Scarf

Finished size: 11" (27.9 cm) wide x 72" (182.9 cm) circumference (37" [94 cm] flat)

Handwork mixes with fresh patchwork for this fanciful scarf.
Wrap yourself in handmade beauty!

NOTES

All seams are ¼" (0.6 cm) unless otherwise stated. The seam allowance is included in all measurements and templates. Press all seam allowances to one side as you sew.

DESIGN INFLUENCES

Flying Geese
Stripes

TECHNIQUES USED

Paper Piecing
Hand Embroidery
Beadwork
Sashiko

Figure 1

Patchwork Section of Scarf

MATERIALS LIST

Fabrics

Use Figure 1 as a guide for selecting the fabrics
From 44" (112 cm) wide light- to mid-weight fabric (unless otherwise noted)

¼ yard (0.23 m) each of 9 coordinating prints and solids for Patchwork Stripes (Optional: Choose one floral print for hand embroidery)

¼ yard (0.23 m) each of 2 coordinating prints or solids for the first stripe of Flying Geese Patchwork

¼ yard (0.23 m) each of 2 coordinating prints or solids for the second stripe of Flying Geese Patchwork

2⅛ yards (1.9 m) of 45" (114 cm) or 60" (152 cm) wide fabric for Scarf (Note: Choose a fabric that is reversible; the Patchwork Panels will only be on one side, but the scarf is not self-lined.)

¼ yard (0.23 m) of coordinating print or solid for Scarf Binding

½ yard (0.46 m) of cotton muslin for Patchwork Backing

OTHER SUPPLIES

1 spool of coordinating all-purpose thread (Coats)

Up to 9 different colors of coordinating all-purpose thread for machine quilting on patchwork strips (Coats)

1 skein of embroidery floss to coordinate with the fabric for one Flying Geese triangle (Anchor by Coats)

2 or 3 skeins of embroidery floss to coordinate with fabric for the hand embroidery (Anchor by Coats)

7" (17.8 cm) embroidery hoop (Clover Embroidery Stitching Tool Hoop)

1 spool of transparent thread

4 beads (4 mm) for embellishment

28 to 30 coordinating seed beads for embellishment

ADDITIONAL TOOLS NEEDED

4 sheets of foundation paper, 9" x 12" (22.9 x 30.5 cm) (Carol Doak's)

Ruler that works with rotary cutter and has ¼" (0.6 cm) markings (such as an Add-A-Quarter Ruler)

1 hand-embroidery needle (Prym-Dritz)

1 short hand-beading needle (Prym-Dritz)

Needle-nose pliers

1 hand-sewing needle

¼" (0.6 cm) piecing foot for your sewing machine

Cut Out the Template Piece

From the pattern sheet included with this book, cut out:
Flying Geese Template

Cut Out the Fabric Pieces

Use your rotary cutter, mat, and ruler to cut the following fabrics:

Flying Geese Stripe 1 (for both Patchwork Panels)

Fabric 1:
Cut 4 squares for Triangles: 4" (10 cm) square
Cut 8 squares for Background: 4" (10 cm) square

Fabric 2:
Cut 4 squares for Triangles: 4" (10 cm) square
Cut 8 squares for Background: 4" (10 cm) square

Flying Geese Stripe 2 (for both Patchwork Panels)

Fabric 3:
Cut 4 squares for Triangles: 4" (10 cm) square
Cut 8 squares for Background: 4" (10 cm) square

Fabric 4:
Cut 4 squares for Triangles: 4" (10 cm) square
Cut 8 squares for Background: 4" (10 cm) square

Patchwork Strip Fabrics

Cut 2 strips from each of the 9 Patchwork Strip fabrics:
Fabric 1: 1¼" x 11¼" (3.2 x 28.6 cm)
Fabric 2: 1" x 11¼" (2.5 x 28.6 cm)
Fabric 3: 1¼" x 11¼" (3.2 x 28.6 cm)
Fabric 4: ⅞" x 11¼" (2.2 x 28.6 cm)
Fabric 5: 1⅞" x 11¼" (4.8 x 28.6 cm)
Fabric 6: 2⅛" x 11¼" (5.4 x 28.6 cm)
Fabric 7: 1⅜" x 11¼" (3.5 x 28.6 cm)
Fabric 8: 1½" x 11¼" (3.8 x 28.6 cm)
Fabric 9: 1⅞" x 11¼" (4.8 x 28.6 cm)

Scarf Fabric

Cut 1 piece: 74" x 11¼" (188 x 28.6 cm)

Binding Fabric

Cut 4 strips: 2" (5 cm) x width of fabric* (wof)

Muslin

Cut 2 pieces: 18" (45.7 cm) square

Make Flying Geese Strips Using Paper Piecing

Note: Each Patchwork Panel has two Flying Geese Strips. The
fabrics in the two strips are reversed on the two panels. (See
Figure 2.)

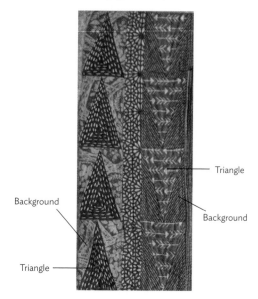

Figure 2

Flying Geese Strips

Triangle

Background

Background

Triangle

The Background and the Triangles are
reversed on second Patchwork Section

a. Trace the Flying Geese Template once onto each piece of
foundation paper, making sure your lines are straight, as you
will be following these lines when you are stitching. Transfer
the numbers of each section onto the tracing.

b. Start with Flying Geese Strip 1 on the first Patchwork Panel.
Place one Flying Geese Triangles square under Section 1
with the **wrong** side against the **wrong** side of the paper.
The fabric piece needs to extend ¼" (0.6 cm) past all sides
of Section 1. Then, take one Background square and match
it with the triangle fabric **right** sides together. Pin these two
layers together through the paper with the paper on top.
Make sure all sides of the fabric pieces extend ¼" (0.6 cm)
past the section outlines. (See Figure 3.)

Figure 3

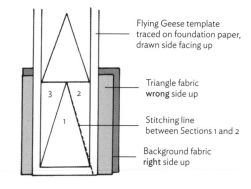

Flying Geese template
traced on foundation paper,
drawn side facing up

Triangle fabric
wrong side up

Stitching line
between Sections 1 and 2

Background fabric
right side up

c. Reduce the stitch length on your sewing machine to 1.5 (12 to 14 stitches/inch/2.5 cm). With the paper side up, stitch along the drawn line between Sections 1 and 2, stitching slightly past the beginning and extending through the seam allowance at the end of the line.

d. Fold the paper back along this stitched line. Use your ruler, rotary cutter, and mat to trim the seam allowance* to ¼" (0.6 cm). (See Figure 4.)

Figure 4

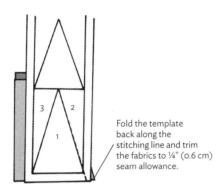

Fold the template back along the stitching line and trim the fabrics to ¼" (0.6 cm) seam allowance.

e. Turn the paper over and press the fabric open with the seam allowances toward Section 2. The background fabric will now be under Section 2. The excess will be cut off later. (See Figure 5.)

Figure 5

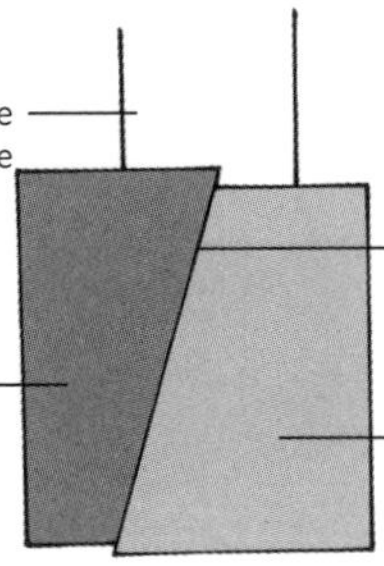

Wrong side of the template

Turn fabric and template over to finger press* along the seam

Background fabric

Triangle fabric

f. Repeat with another square of the background fabric for Section 3 on the other side. (See Figures 6 and 7.)

Figure 6

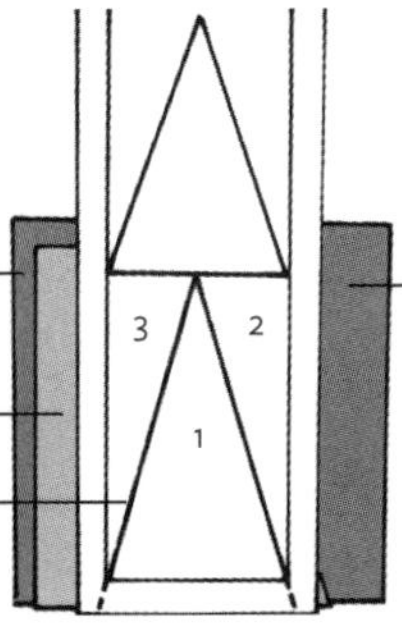

Background fabric for Section 3

Triangle fabric

Stitching line between Sections 1 and 3

Wrong side of Background fabric over Section 2

Figure 7

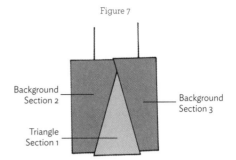

Background Section 2

Background Section 3

Triangle Section 1

Right side of first Flying Geese Section

g. Place the second Flying Geese Triangle fabric square **right** sides together against this first block you just made. Pin through the layers to hold. With the paper side facing up, stitch along the line at the bottom of Section 4.

h. Fold the paper back along this stitched line. Trim the seam allowance to ¼" (0.6 cm). Turn the paper over and press the fabric open with the seam allowance going toward Section 4.

i. Repeat Steps 3b to 3f to sew the background fabrics for Sections 5 and 6 to both sides of the Flying Geese Section 4. Then complete the remaining two Flying Geese sections in this strip.

j. Trim along the outside edges of the template and gently remove the paper.

k. Repeat Steps 3b to 3j to complete Flying Geese Strip 1 for Patchwork Panel 2, alternating the fabrics for the Flying Geese Triangles and the Background. Then make two Flying Geese Strip 2 pieces, alternating the fabrics.

 Make the Patchwork Panels

a. Divide the Patchwork and Flying Geese Strips into two groups for the Patchwork Panels.

b. Start with the first panel and follow the layout in Figure 1 to lay the strips in order.

c. Working from the left to right, pin the long edges of the first two strips **right** sides together. Sew the strips together and press the seam allowances in one direction.

d. Pin the next strip, **right** sides together, onto the previous strip and stitch. Continue pinning and sewing in the same manner to complete the panel.

e. Repeat Steps 4b to 4d to make the second Patchwork Panel.

 Quilt and Embellish the Patchwork Panel

a. Center the **wrong** side of the first Patchwork Panel on one muslin piece. The muslin will be larger than the panel. Smooth out any wrinkles and pin in place.

b. For the sashiko stitching on the Flying Geese:

Place the panel and muslin in the quilting hoop, centering it on the first triangle, making sure there is at least 1" (2.5 cm) of fabric outside of the hoop at all times.

Thread your hand-embroidery needle with two or three strands of embroidery floss. Tie a knot at one end.

With your chalk pencil and ruler, mark the sashiko lines on the triangle following the image in Figure 8.

Bring the needle up, from the **wrong** side to the right, at one of the marked stitches. Make a single straight stitch about ⅛" to ³⁄₁₆" (0.3 to 0.4 cm) long, following the drawn lines. Space your stitches evenly and the rows of stitches ¹⁄₁₆" to ⅛" (0.1 to 0.3 cm) apart. Make a knot on the **wrong** side of the fabric with the last stitch.

Repeat to stitch the remaining three Flying Geese triangles in this Strip, moving the hoop as necessary.

Figure 8

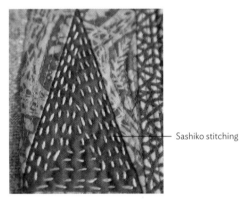

Sashiko stitching

c. For the hand embroidery (use Figure 9 as a guide):

You will use a satin stitch* to fill in patterns on one of the print fabrics. I chose a floral print. Choose small elements of the print that you would like to highlight. Re-hoop the panel and muslin over the portion of the strip you wish to embroider, making sure there is at least 1" (2.5 cm) of fabric outside of the hoop at all times.

Thread your hand-embroidery needle with three strands of embroidery floss. Tie a knot at one end.

Start in the center of the pattern. Bring the needle up from the **wrong** side of the fabric on the outside edge of the pattern. Reinsert your needle into the fabric directly across from where you brought it up through the fabric, spanning the pattern. Pull the thread taut, but don't make the fabric pucker.

Bring the needle up next to the original stitch and make a second stitch parallel to the first with very little gap between the two. Continue sewing in this manner to cover the entire motif. Tie a knot on the back of fabric when you are finished.

Re-thread your needle and continue satin stitching any other areas of the patchwork strip you wish to fill in on both panels.

Figure 9

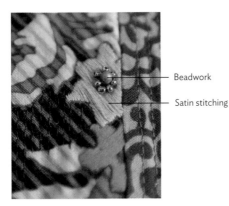

Beadwork

Satin stitching

Hand embroidery on fabric print

d. For the beadwork (use Figure 9 as a guide):

Select design details on a floral print or other fabric to embellish with bead clusters. Note: The beadwork does not have to be done inside the embroidery hoop.

Thread your beading needle with a double strand of transparent thread and tie a knot at the end. Tip: Kink the thread with a pair of needle-nose pliers where you want the knot to go. When you tie the knot at this kink, it will be less likely to shift. Use the pliers to help pull the knot tight.

Stitch a large bead in the middle of a chosen design. Then, stitch six or seven small beads around central large bead.

Repeat for a second bead cluster on the first panel. Repeat to make two bead clusters on the second panel.

e. For the machine quilting (use Figure 10 as a guide):

Thread your machine with the appropriate thread for each Patchwork Panel and Flying Geese Strip as you work.

Attach your ¼" (0.6 cm) piecing foot and set your stitch length slightly longer than normal.

Start with the Patchwork Strips by sewing lines ¼" (0.6 cm) apart down each strip. Go back and stitch between each row of stitching so the rows end up being ⅛" (0.3 cm) apart and the panel has a flat feel. Note: For the strips with the hand embroidery, stitch in the areas that are not embroidered, working around the embroidered areas.

Follow the stitching guide in Figure 10 for the Flying Geese Strips, keeping the stitches ⅛" (0.3 cm) apart on the background fabric and ¼" (0.6 cm) apart inside the Flying Geese Triangles.

Figure 10

⅛" (0.3 cm) rows of stitching on each strip

 Construct the Scarf

a. Match the short ends of the Scarf fabric, **wrong** sides together, and stitch. Press the seam allowance open.

b. Place the **wrong** side of the first Patchwork Panel onto the Scarf so that one short end completely covers the seam and seam allowance. Pin the Panel onto the Scarf.

c. Place the second Patchwork Panel 28" (71.1 cm) to the right of the first Panel. Pin the Panel to the Scarf. Try on the Scarf, looping for two layers, and adjust the placement of both panels to your liking. Carefully remove the Scarf.

d. With your chalk pencil, mark the placement of both Patchwork Panels and then unpin them from the Scarf. Press each short end under ¼" (0.6 cm) to the **wrong** side on both panels. Repin the panels to the Scarf where marked.

e. Use a hand-sewing needle and thread to slipstitch* the Panels to the Scarf along all short ends on both Patchwork Panels, hiding your stitches.

Sew the Binding* to the Scarf

a. Sew the Binding strips together along the short ends and then trim to make two long strips that are 2" (5.1 cm) wide x 74" (188.0 cm) long.

b. Follow the steps for French Straight Binding* in the Glossary and Techniques section (page 166) to finish the Scarf.

c. Wash the scarf when you are finished to soften the fabrics.

Bijoux Belt

Finished sizes: XS – XXXL • Finished dimensions for Belt Band:

Note: This belt is sized for the high hip. Measurements are given based on the following dimensions. Follow the directions given to alter the length of the Belt Band for a personal fit. XS: 32½" x 2" (82.6 x 5.1 cm) • S: 34½" x 2" (87.6 x 5.1 cm) • M: 36" x 2" (91.4 x 5.1 cm) L: 38" x 2" (96.5 x 5.1 cm) • XL: 42" x 2" (106.7 x 5.1 cm) • XXL: 45" x 2" (114.3 x 5.1 cm) • XXXL: 47" x 2" (119.4 x 5.1 cm)

It's time to spice up your wardrobe! Beautiful handwork and beading add richness and texture to this unique patchwork belt.

NOTES

All seams are ¼" (0.6 cm) unless otherwise stated. The seam allowance is included in all measurements. Press all seam allowances to one side as you sew.

DESIGN INFLUENCE

Wonky Log Cabin

TECHNIQUES USED

Patchwork
Beadwork
Suffolk Puffs

Figure 1

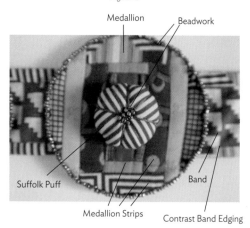

Medallion
Beadwork
Suffolk Puff
Medallion Strips
Band
Contrast Band Edging

MATERIALS LIST

Fabrics

Use Figure 1 as a guide
From 44" (112 cm) wide light- to mid-weight fabric
⅛ yard (0.11 m) each of 7 coordinating prints for the Medallion Strips
⅛ yard (0.11 m) of coordinating print for the Suffolk Puffs
¼ yard (0.23 m) of coordinating solid or print for the Medallion Backing
¼ yard (0.23 m) of coordinating print for the Belt Band (all sizes)
¼ yard (0.23 m) of coordinating print for the Contrasting Band Edging and Ties

OTHER SUPPLIES

⅛ yard (0.11 m) of 20" (50.8 cm) wide fusible Peltex (Pellon 71F)
1 spool of coordinating all-purpose thread (Coats)
1 spool of transparent thread
1 skein of coordinating embroidery floss (Anchor by Coats)
Small gold seed beads (approximately 660 beads)

ADDITIONAL TOOLS NEEDED

Masking tape and marker
Turning tool
1 short beading needle (Prym-Dritz)
Needle-nose pliers
1 standard hand-sewing needle
8 jumbo-size cotton balls
1 long hand-embroidery needle (Prym-Dritz)

1 Cut Out the Template Pieces

From the pattern sheet included with this book, cut out:
Medallion
Suffolk Puff

2 Cut Out the Fabric Pieces

Use your rotary cutter, mat, and ruler to cut the specific amounts listed below.

Medallion Strips

Lay your seven coordinating fabrics out in front of you and decide on their order, using Figure 1 as a guide. Use the masking tape and marker to number the fabrics to keep track of their order.
Cut 4 strips from Fabric 1 – 1" x 2½" (2.5 x 6.4 cm)
Cut 8 strips from Fabric 2 – ¾" x 2½" (1.9 x 6.4 cm)
Cut 8 strips from Fabric 3 – ¾" x 1½" (1.9 x 3.8 cm)
Cut 8 strips from Fabric 4 – 1" x 3" (2.5 x 7.6 cm)
Cut 8 strips from Fabric 5 – 1" x 2½" (2.5 x 6.4 cm)
Cut 8 strips from Fabric 6 – ⅞" x 4" (2.2 x 10.2 cm)
Cut 8 strips from Fabric 7 – 1" x 4" (2.5 x 10.2 cm)

Medallion Backing

Cut 4 pieces – 4½" (11.4 cm) square

Belt Band

For sizes XS – L:

From the fabric for the Belt Band, cut a strip 2" (5 cm) wide to the length specified, or measure where you'd like the belt to fit and add 2½" (6.5 cm).

XS – 35" (88.9 cm), S – 37" (94 cm), M – 38½" (97.8 cm), L – 40½" (102.9 cm)

From the Backing fabric, cut a strip 2½" (6.5 cm) wide to the same measurement as your Belt Band.

For sizes XL – XXXL:

From the fabric for the Belt Band, cut two strips 2" (5 cm) wide to the length specified, or measure where you'd like the belt to fit, add 3½" (9 cm), then divide by 2 and cut two lengths to this measurement.

XL – 22¾" (57.8 cm), XXL – 24¼" (61.6 cm), XXXL – 25¼" (64.1 cm)

* From the fabric for the Backing, cut two strips 2½" (6.2 cm) x Cutting Length of the previous step.

Contrasting Band Edging

For all sizes, cut one strip: ¾" (1.9 cm) x Cutting Length measurement used above

Ties

Cut 2 ties: 2½" x 18½" (6.2 x 47 cm)

Suffolk Puff

Cut 4 pieces, using template

Peltex

Cut 4 pieces: 4½" (11.4 cm) square
Cut 4: 1" (2.5 cm) diameter circles

3 Make the Patchwork Front for the Medallions

Note: Use Figure 2 as a guide for sewing the strips.

Figure 2
Patchwork for Medallion

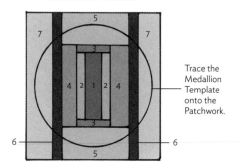

Trace the Medallion Template onto the Patchwork.

a. Starting with the first Medallion, take one strip of Fabric 1 and one strip of Fabric 2 and pin the **right** sides together along two of the long edges. Stitch along the pinned edges and press the seam toward Fabric 2.

b. Pin a second strip of Fabric 2 to the opposite side of Fabric 1 with **right** sides together and stitch along the pinned edges. Press the seam toward Fabric 2.

c. Pin the first strip of Fabric 3 to the top short edge of the Fabric 2/1/2 block. Stitch along the pinned edges. Press the seam toward Fabric 3. Repeat with a second Fabric 3 strip on the opposite end.

d. Take one strip of Fabric 4 and pin it, with the **right** sides together, to one long edge of the block along the Fabric 2 and 3 strips. Stitch along the pinned edges. Press the seam toward Fabric 4. Repeat on the opposite side with a second strip of Fabric 4.

e. Referring to Figure 2, continue in the same manner to attach Strips 5, 6, and 7.

f. Center the Medallion pattern piece over the patchwork block. Trace around the pattern with a chalk pencil or marking pen, and then cut along the drawn line.

g. Repeat Steps 2a to 2f for the other three patchwork blocks.

4 Make the Medallions

a. Fuse one Peltex piece to the **wrong** side of one Backing piece. Cut a 2½" (6.4 cm) long slit the center of the Backing piece through the fabric and the Peltex. Repeat for the other three Backing and Peltex pieces.

b. Next, center one Patchwork Medallion onto one Backing piece, **right** sides together, positioning the slit on the Backing piece so it runs horizontal to the piecing on the Medallion as shown in Figure 2. Pin together.

c. Stitch slowly around the outside edge of the circle in a smooth, gentle curve. Trim the excess Backing so it is even with the edge of the circle. Trim the seam allowance* to ⅛" (0.3 cm) and clip* along the curves, being careful not to cut the stitching.

d. Gently turn the Medallion **right** side out through the slit in the Backing. Use a turning tool* to push out the edges. Press well along the edges.

e. Stitch-in-the-ditch* along the patchwork seams with transparent thread in your needle.

f. Thread your beading needle with a double strand of transparent thread and tie a knot at the end. Tip: Kink the thread with a pair of needle-nose pliers where you want the knot to go. When you tie the knot at this kink, it will be less likely to shift. Use the pliers to help pull the knot tight. Pull the needle through the opening in the Backing and up through the outside seam in order to hide the knot. Take a few stitches through the fabric to secure your starting point.

g. Hand stitch the seed beads close together around the outside edge of the Medallion. Work with one to three beads at a time, pushing the beads down to where the thread comes through the seam. Push the needle back into the fabric through the hole where the thread came out. Make sure to pull tight enough on the threads so that the beads are touching the fabric.

h. Come back up through the edge near where you ended stitching the previous set of beads and pass the needle back through the last bead in the set. Thread the needle again with one to three beads, and repeat the previous step to bead around the entire Medallion. When you finish, take a few stitches in one place and tie a knot.

i. Complete the remaining three Medallions the same way.

Make the Suffolk Puffs

a. Thread your hand-sewing needle with two strands of thread, bring the ends together, and make a knot. Take one Suffolk Puff fabric circle and starting and stopping on the **right** side of the fabric, sew a running stitch* around the circumference ¼" (0.6 cm) from the raw edge.

b. Pull the needle end of the thread to gently gather the edge of the circle, creating a little pouch.

c. Place one cotton ball into the pouch. Then layer on top of it one of the 1" (2.5 cm) Peltex circles and another cotton ball. Pull the needle end of the thread tightly to close the fabric pouch around the cotton balls with the edges of the fabric completely covering them. Secure the thread by sewing a couple of stitches in place, cutting the thread close to the puff.

d. Divide the puff into eight even, pie-shaped sections by marking with a chalk pencil or marking pen.

e. Thread the hand-embroidery needle with four strands of embroidery floss and knot the end.

f. Pierce the bottom center of the puff and bring your needle up through the center top where all the drawn lines intersect. Then following one of the drawn lines, wrap the floss around the diameter of the puff, and push the needle back down through the puff in the same hole, from the top to the bottom. Pull the floss tight to slightly dimple the top.

g. Laying the floss along another one of the drawn lines, push the needle from the top to the bottom through the same center hole. (Only half of the puff will be covered.) Pull tight to dimple. Continue in the same manner until all of the drawn lines are covered. Stitch in place a couple of times on the bottom to secure the floss. Make a knot at the bottom and cut close to the knot.

h. With a beading needle and transparent thread, hand sew ten seed beads in a tight cluster at the center top of the puff. Hide the knot on the bottom of the puff.

i. Hand sew the puff to the center of one Medallion by securely stitching around the puff circumference and through to the back of the Medallion.

j. Repeat Steps 4a to 4g with the remaining three Suffolk Puffs and Medallions.

 Make the Ties

a. Press the first Tie in half lengthwise, **wrong** sides together, then open up. Now, fold the raw edges toward the pressed crease and press again. Turn one short end ¼" (0.6 cm) toward the **wrong** side and press.

b. Fold the Tie in half again along the original crease and press. Pin the folded edges together and then edge stitch* along the pinned edges.

c. Repeat for the second Tie.

 Make the Band

a. For sizes XL – XXXL, pin the one short edge of the two Band pieces together and sew. Press the seam open. Repeat on the Contrast Band Edging and Backing pieces.

b. Pin the long edge of one Contrast Band Edging strip to one long edge of the Band, **right** sides together. Stitch the seam and turn the piece **right** side up. Press the seam flat toward the raw edge of the Contrast Band Edging. Repeat with the second edging strip on the other side of the Band.

c. Pin the Band and the Backing, **right** sides together, matching all the edges. Stitch along both long edges, leaving the short ends unstitched. Turn the Band **right** side out through one of the short ends.

d. Fold under both short ends ½" (1.3 cm) toward the inside of the Band, and press. Tuck the raw end of one Tie 1" (2.5 cm) into the opening on one end of the Band, centering the Tie. Edge stitch the opening closed, securing the Tie in place. Repeat on the other end of the Band with the second Tie.

 Complete the Belt

a. Find the center of the Belt by folding it in half and mark with a pin on the **right** side. Fold the Belt in half again to find the quarter measurement, and mark both ends with pins. Open the Belt and place it in front of you with the **right** side facing up, repositioning the pins to the **right** side if necessary. (See Figure 3.)

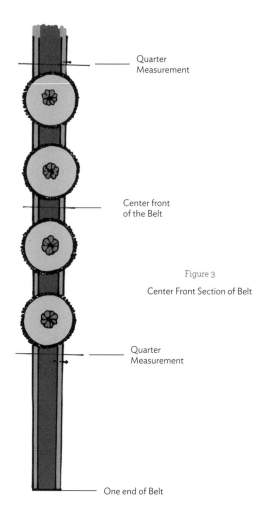

Figure 3
Center Front Section of Belt

Quarter Measurement

Center front of the Belt

Quarter Measurement

One end of Belt

b. Position the Medallions evenly between the two outside pins, with two on each side of the center pin. Pin the Medallions in place and try the Belt on. Adjust the Medallion placing if necessary.

c. Use a needle and transparent thread to hand stitch the Medallions onto the Belt, making sure the Medallions are turned so that the slit is covered by the Belt.

Creative Communion

The Importance of Keeping Your Creative Fires Burning

Has your creative fire been put on the back burner? Our time communing with our creativity is one of the most important things we can do for ourselves, and ultimately, for others. It's time to tap into crafty resources and get your mojo flowing!

Creative Communion

I wanted to share about creative communion because it's the glue that keeps us inspired and happy. I know personally if I don't carve out creative "me time" it doesn't happen. And sadly, this is one of the first things to go when we prioritize the activities in our busy lives. I know what you're thinking: "But Amy, you get to be creative with your business every day. Don't you make a living by making art? Isn't that enough to fulfill you?" The answer is yes . . . and no. I'm greatly fulfilled by my creative work, and I love what I do, but what I create in unscheduled hours is just for me. There are no deadlines involved, no schedules to keep, no files to share . . . it's just pure crafting, creating, and hand-making. I liken it to active meditation. It's those times when you are creating and you lose total track of time, you get lost in what you are doing and you are transported into a state of bliss. This state is what I call my creative mojo. When I am in this place, I am generating incredible amounts of creative energy that becomes a sustaining resource that keeps me jazzed and inspired for months. It's a tether to my soul, and when I make time to connect to it, all areas in my life are elevated. In this place I'm happy, fulfilled, excited, and open! This is why we love to create, and, when we don't allow ourselves to take the time to do so, we suffer—feeling blocked, lackluster, and a bit disconnected from life.

Crafty Weekends

But how do we get back to connecting with our creative mojo if we haven't been taking the time to do so? Sometimes it can feel overwhelming, but I've discovered great resources that have supported me tremendously—like hosting crafty weekends and taking part in life-coaching events for creatives. My Crafty Weekends came about out of sheer hunger for both creative time and communion with my friends. Before I started hosting, I set up some ground rules so it didn't turn into a crazy event for the host, and so that it would be super easy for everyone to say YES! That part is not so hard. What I've discovered is that we're all looking for an opportunity to get our craft on. And you can easily do this with your friends or friends-to-be!

My Crafty Weekend Rules

It has to be EASY and low impact on the host. The idea is to remove as many roadblocks as possible that could become excuses later to keep you from having the gathering. Once or twice I almost canceled because I felt tired and rundown, but then I remembered how good it feels after I take part in the weekends and also how simple it is because my friends are helping with the food and supplies. This is a perfect scenario! The host doesn't do a stitch of cooking and everyone pitches in. Here's the list I share with everyone before they come for the weekend. Bring:

- Yourself and your sleeping stuff—pillow and sleeping bag, a towel (for bathtime and hot tub!)

- Art, craft, and sewing supplies, and a machine if you like. Think jewelry-making materials, paints, yarn for knitting, ribbons, and fabric!

- Drinks of choice

- Fresh, healthy food to share for easy noshing

The beauty of communal supplies is that you end up experimenting with interesting craft materials and food! I've learned all kinds of new techniques and how to make myriad sewing and craft projects, and many have become huge inspirations for my creative business and workshops.

These Crafty Weekends are the modern version of the old-fashioned quilting bee. The time bonding with other women is so precious and important. We catch up on everyone's lives, laugh a lot, and get pretty silly. Don't be fooled, though—it's quite a productive session. Many evenings turn into early mornings because we find it so hard to stop and go to sleep. When these weekends close I am creatively full, happy, and inspired, and the great flux of energy and ideas stay with me for months. Dare I say, these gatherings have become quite addictive? Remember, you can create the kind of weekend or overnight that works for you. I reckon it wouldn't take much to convince a few of your friends to join in. Rotate hosting so each of you has a weekend planned. Before you know it, you

Easy . . .

will have created a wonderful tradition that flows through your year, with lots of opportunities to fill yourself up creatively!

Design Your Life Weekends and Dreaming in Color Workshops

I have experienced the same delicious bonding, growth, and communion taking part in events with my friends at Handel Life Coaching by attending their Design Your Life weekend events and through the Dreaming in Color workshops that I lead with my friend Hildie, a senior coach at Handel. I've been coaching with Hildie for four years, and this work has been paramount in removing creative blocks and powerfully getting me into action around my creative time, priorities, and career. The methodology provides a wonderful tool kit that I've used for removing the bits and bobs I've been processing in my head from long years of conditioning that don't serve me. I've been able to get perspective in every aspect of my life. What I love about my Handel work is that it's been step by step and has gently and clearly opened my heart and mind to the truth. It has put me into action, supporting my dreams and intentions, and allowed me to see the possibilities that exist. I think these sorts of opportunities are available and meant for all of us! And that's why I LOVE sharing about this work. Here are a few details on my Dreaming in Color workshops and Handel.

Dreaming in Color Workshops

During these dynamic workshops, I lead you through fabulous creative projects that connect you to your heart, too. Hildie helps you discover your dreams for your life as you learn how to tell the truth about what you really want while dismantling the fears that are holding you back. You leave this workshop empowered and tapped into your unique creative spirit!

For more information:

www.amybutlerdesign.com/workshops_seminars

Handel Life Coaching

For powerful one-on-one coaching, group events, and Design Your Life weekends. www.handelgroup.com

Be Inspired! Reach Out and Touch Someone—Share Your Gifts, Projects, and Love

There are also times when you're in the moment and you just need a quick inspiration boost, and thank goodness we live in a world where we can easily access resources and connections through fantastic websites, blogs, magazines, and social media. Reaching out to connect with someone has never been easier. Sometimes you just need five minutes on a social site or with a beautiful blog to find that creative spark. And how wonderful it is to be able to meet like-minded creative souls from around the globe! Here are a few of my favorite online resources that offer great inspiration, but also the opportunity to share *your* creations—paying forward your awesome mojo that will no doubt inspire many others!

Blossom Magazine—free online and printed annually by Chronicle Books

This is my visual journal that's all about loving your life and living it fully and authentically. Filled with loads of creative ideas and inspirations, *Blossom* celebrates our collective creative expression and passion. It's my dream to help folks get in touch with the beauty in their lives and in themselves, to empower with love, and to help people connect with the creative perfection of being who they really are. My *Blossom* motto is Create Love, Express Beauty, and Be Kind.
Visit www.amybutlerdesign.com/blossommagazine.

Sharing and Learning Sources

Pinterest.com—An endless source of inspiration and a great spot to share what you're making.
Flickr.com—A wonderful photo-sharing site where you can easily search for groups that have similar interests.
Kollabora.com—An amazing online community where you can browse for inspirational projects, shop for supplies, and share your own projects.
Ravelry.com—The best resource for folks who love knitting and crochet. You can search through their inspirational projects and share your creations.
Crafster.org—An online community where people share hip, offbeat, crafty DIY projects. There's lots of inspiration, online classes, and great message boards, too.

Meetup.com—Search for people who share your interests in your area. Or start your own group to meet new friends!

TheModernQuiltGuild.com—A nationwide resource for finding local modern guilds in your area, offering great opportunities to learn, share, and connect with others.

Creative Conferences and Workshops

The Makerie—www.themakerie.com

Quiltcon—www.quiltcon.com

French General—www.frenchgeneral.com

Online Classes

www.creativebug.com

www.craftdaily.com

www.creativelive.com

www.craftsy.com

No matter how your find your juice, mojo, or creative fire, taking time out to honor and express that very special part of who you are not only makes your life richer and fuller but also your happiness flows over into every life you touch. If you ever need a buddy or an enabler (call it what you will), know you will always have my love and support on your side. Craft ON and make the world a better place!

Glossary and Techniques

Appliqué

This is a technique where one piece of fabric is sewn onto another piece of fabric for decorative purposes. A tight zigzag called a satin stitch is usually used to appliqué on a sewing machine. An invisible stitch is used when sewing by hand, taking a short stitch through the appliqué and then another in the foundation fabric.

Assembling the Quilt

a. Trim any selvages from the Backing Panels and pin them **right** sides together along the long edges. Sew along the pinned edges, using a ½" (1.3 cm) seam allowance. Press the seam allowances open.

b. Place the Back Panel **wrong** side up on a large, flat surface and smooth out any wrinkles.

c. Place the batting on top of the Back Panel and smooth out the wrinkles.

d. Center the Quilt Top **right** side up on the top of the batting, creating a sandwich of the Back Panel, batting, and Quilt Top, and smooth out the wrinkles. Note: The batting and the Back Panel are larger than the Quilt Top.

e. To hold the pieces together as you quilt, use safety pins to pin the layers together every 8" to 10" (20 to 25 cm) or hand baste the layers together, making a series of long, running stitches through all of the layers.

f. Machine or hand quilt as desired, starting at the center of the quilt and working your way to the outside edges.

g. Lay the quilt on a large, flat surface with the Quilt Top facing up. Using your ruler, fabric marker, and scissors (or a rotary cutter, ruler, and mat), measure and mark 1" (2.5 cm) from the outside edges of the pieced blocks on the first raw edge, then draw a line connecting the marks, extending your line to the quilt's edges. Repeat to draw a line along each edge.

h. Cut along the marked lines, trimming the excess Back Panel, batting, and Quilt Top.

i. Hand or machine baste ⅛" (0.3 cm) from the raw edges to secure the three layers together before attaching your Binding. Remove the safety pins or basting stitches.

Backstitch

This is used to reinforce your stitching and keep it from unraveling. To do this, put your machine in the reverse position and make three or four stitches.

Bartack

To bartack, use the widest zigzag stitch on your sewing machine and sew a few times in place to secure a seam or the end of a zipper.

Baste

See *Hand Baste* or *Machine Baste*.

Bias

See *Fabric Grain*.

Binding

Binding is a strip of fabric cut on the bias or across the width of the fabric. It is used to cover the raw edges of a project, such as a quilt. Here are instructions for two different types of binding you might use.

French Bias Binding

a. Place the fabric on a large, flat surface, **right** side facing up. Fold one selvage edge over to meet the cut edge, forming a triangle shape. Press a crease on the fold. Open the fabric and cut along the creased line. (See Figure 1.)

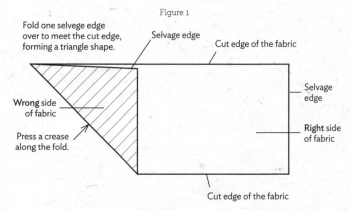

Figure 1

Fold one selvage edge over to meet the cut edge, forming a triangle shape.

Selvage edge

Cut edge of the fabric

Wrong side of fabric

Press a crease along the fold.

Selvage edge

Right side of fabric

Cut edge of the fabric

b. Starting at one end of the bias edge, measure in the distance instructed in the project, and parallel to the edge, and make a mark. Make another mark the same distance in from the opposite end. Match the two marks and draw a line using a ruler and fabric marker to create a bias strip. Continue to measure and mark more strips until you have the length called for in the project's instructions. Cut along the marked lines. (See Figure 2.)

Figure 2

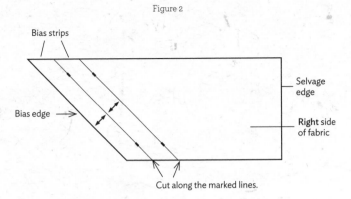

Bias strips

Selvage edge

Bias edge →

Right side of fabric

Cut along the marked lines.

c. Attach the strips into one long, continuous piece: Place two strips perpendicular to each other, with the **right** sides together, matching the short ends, and pin them in place. Stitch a ¼" (0.6 cm) seam across the pinned edge and backstitch at each end. Trim the seam allowance to ¼" (0.6 cm), press the seam allowance open, and trim any fabric tails that hang over the edge of the bias strip. Repeat until you have created a strip the length required for the project. (See Figure 3.)

Figure 3

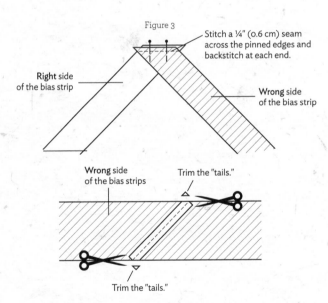

Stitch a ¼" (0.6 cm) seam across the pinned edges and backstitch at each end.

Right side of the bias strip

Wrong side of the bias strip

Wrong side of the bias strips

Trim the "tails."

Trim the "tails."

d. Fold the strip in half lengthwise with the **wrong** sides together. Match the long edges and press a crease along the fold.

e. Beginning in the center front of the project, match the raw edges of the strip with the edge of the project, **right** sides together. Pin it in place. Begin sewing a couple of inches in from the first end and stitch a ½" (1.3 cm) seam, stopping ½" (1.3 cm) in from the first corner. Backstitch at each end.

f. Miter the corners. Stop stitching ½" (1.3 cm) from the corner, backstitch, and remove the project from the sewing machine. To form a neatly mitered corner, fold the binding perpendicular, away from the corner, forming a 45-degree angle as shown in Figure 4. Now, fold it straight down even with the next edge to be sewn and pin it in place. Leave the fold on the binding even with the first edge that was sewn.

Figure 4

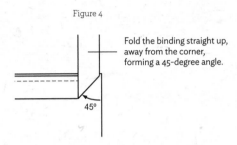

Fold the binding straight up, away from the corner, forming a 45-degree angle.

45°

g. Begin stitching again at the corner, and backstitch as you begin. Sew along the pinned edge, stopping ½" (1.3 cm) in from the next corner. Repeat this process to attach the binding to the remaining edges and corners. (See Figure 5.)

Figure 5

Now fold the binding straight down even with the next edge to be sewn.

Leave the fold on the binding even with the first edge that was sewn.

Begin stitching at the corner and backstitch as you begin.

h. Stop stitching about 4" (10 cm) from the first end of the binding. Cut the binding so it overlaps the beginning by 1½" (3.8 cm). Fold the first end ½" (1.3 cm) back and press. Place the second end over the first and pin it in place. Continue to sew the last inches of the binding to the quilt, backstitching at each end. Note: Once the binding is turned to the other side of the project, the beginning fold will hide the raw edge. (See Figure 6.)

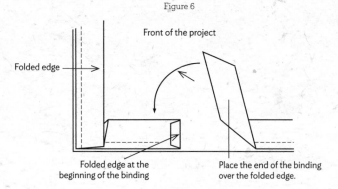

Figure 6

Front of the project

Folded edge

Folded edge at the beginning of the binding

Place the end of the binding over the folded edge.

i. Turn the project over so the back is facing up. Flip the binding over from front to back. Line up the folded edge so it just covers the stitching line that attached it to the front. Adjust the mitered corners and pin them in place. Slipstitch along the inner folded edge, folding the corners to create mitered corners. (See Figure 7.)

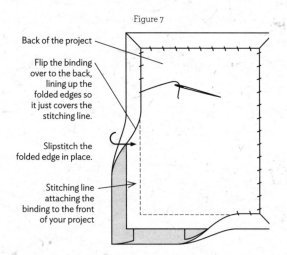

Figure 7

Back of the project

Flip the binding over to the back, lining up the folded edges so it just covers the stitching line.

Slipstitch the folded edge in place.

Stitching line attaching the binding to the front of your project

French Straight Binding

a. Cut strips for binding across the width of the fabric, until you have enough for the length called for in the pattern instructions.

b. Follow the instructions for Step 1c in the "French Bias Binding" except match the top left corner of one strip with the top right corner of the next strip and sew diagonally across the edges. Then cut across the corners, leaving a ¼" (0.6 cm) on the outside of the stitching line to create a seam allowance.

c. Follow Steps 1d to 1i in the "French Bias Binding" to attach the binding, miter the corners, finish the ends, and sew the binding to the other side of the project.

Clip

Clipping allows some give in your seam allowance, especially if it is curved, in order to make the seam lie flat and make it easier to turn your project **right** side out. When clipping, use your scissors to cut into the seam allowance only, making cuts up to the stitch line but taking care not to cut your stitching.

Crosswise Grain

See *Fabric Grain*.

Dots on Pattern Pieces

Dots are used as guidelines for starting and stopping when you are stitching pieces together or as pivot points to stop and turn your project before you continue sewing. Dots can also identify where you should end a clip in a seam allowance. Transfer the dot onto the **wrong** side of the fabric by marking its position with your chalk pencil.

Edge Stitch

An edge stitch is a very narrow stitch done by machine sewing close to the edge or seam to finish a project, close an opening, or stitch something in place.

Embroidery Stitches

Backstitch

First mark the shape as a guide for your stitches on the **right** side of your fabric. Using one to three strands of embroidery floss, insert your needle up through point A and down through point B. Then bring your needle up at point C and down again through point A. Continue in this manner to the end of your marked line. Tie off your stitches with a knot on the back of your fabric. (See Figure 8.)

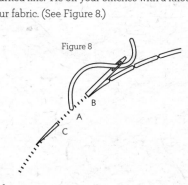

Figure 8

B
A
C

Running Stitch

First mark a line as a guide for your stitches on the **right** side of your fabric. Using one to three strands of embroidery floss, insert your needle up through point A and down through point B. Then bring your needle up at point C and down through point D. Continue in this manner, keeping your spaces and stitches even, to the end of your marked line. Tie off your stitches with a knot on the back of your fabric. (See Figure 9.)

Figure 9

— Running stitch

Satin Stitch

First mark the shape on the **right** side of your fabric as a guide for your stitches. Using one to three strands of embroidery floss, insert your needle up at point A and down though point B. Bring your needle up through point C and repeat, keeping each stitch very close to the previous one. Tie off your stitches with a knot on the back of your fabric. (See Figure 10.)

Figure 10

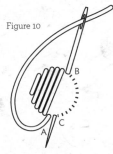

Fabric Grain

Most fabric is made of lengthwise threads woven at right angles with a set of crosswise threads. Grain indicates the direction of these threads. Lengthwise grain (also called straight of grain) refers to the lengthwise threads, or the fabric's length parallel to the selvage edge. Crosswise grain refers to the crosswise threads, or the fabric's width, and runs across the fabric from selvage to selvage. Bias refers to any diagonal line. The bias fold refers to the diagonal fold on a rectangle of fabric aligning two adjacent sides of the cloth, producing a 45-degree angle. This is an effective way to mark and cut bias strips.

Finger Press

To finger press you use your finger or thumbnail to make a crease along an edge or seam, often when an iron cannot be used. It is also a gentler way to press areas that are on the bias to keep them from stretching.

Free-Motion Quilting

Free motion quilting refers to stitching on a sewing machine with the feed teeth dropped or covered and a darning or free-motion presser foot in place of a standard foot. Because the feed teeth are not pulling the fabric layers through the machine, the sewer guides the layers to create a design.

Fussy Cut

To carefully cut out a particular design or desired section of a larger piece of fabric instead of just randomly cutting into the fabric.

Grain

See *Fabric Grain*.

Gusset

A gusset is used to give depth to an otherwise flat piece, for example, the bottom of a purse. To make a gusset, fold a triangle toward the bottom of your bag, with the side seam and bottom seam (or center crease) aligned. Sew across the corner at a 45-degree angle, as instructed for your project.

Hand Baste

Basting is used to temporarily hold two pieces of fabric together to prevent shifting while sewing final stitches. Basting can be done with pins, a sewing machine, or by hand. To hand baste, place the two pieces of fabric in the desired position. Then make a series of long, running stitches in the area described in the pattern instructions.

Interfacing

A stiff, fabric-like material, either woven, nonwoven, or knit, used to give your project strength and durability. Interfacing also gives lighter weight fabrics form and body. Interfacings can be fusible (iron-on) or sewn-in, both of which come in various weights. If you buy fusible interfacing, be sure to follow the manufacturer's instructions to correctly fuse it in place. Any woven interfacing should be preshrunk before using.

Machine Baste

A machine basting stitch is used to hold sections of your project in place until you are ready to complete your final stitches. Use the longest stitch on your sewing machine so you can easily remove these basting stitches later. Do not backstitch at either end of your stitching.

"On the Fold"

To cut a pattern piece on the fold, place it on the fabric with the marked side even with the folded edge of the fabric. Once the fabric piece is cut out, open it up to make one full-size panel.

Overcast Stitch

An overcast stitch is a sewing machine stitch used to finish raw edges and prevent them from raveling. Any zigzag stitch can be used for overcasting.

Pivot

Pivoting is used when you reach a corner or any place where you want to turn and continue stitching in a different direction. To pivot, stop stitching, keep your fabric in place, make sure the needle is in the down position, pick up the presser foot, and rotate your fabric to continue stitching in a different direction.

Press

Using an iron and ironing board, press your fabric after you prewash it to remove all wrinkles and creases. This is an important part of making your project. Any wrinkles or creases on your fabric when cutting out pattern pieces can distort your fabric panel. Also, press the seam allowances open or to one side as you sew them. This will make your finished project look neat and well constructed.

Pressing Cloth

A pressing cloth is a lightweight, neutral fabric placed between your project and the iron to protect your material from scorching. You can also use a damp cloth to sharply press seams and creases.

Seam Allowance

A seam allowance is the distance from the stitching line to the cut edge of the fabric. This extra fabric can be pressed open or to one side, as indicated in the project directions. If a pattern states a ¼" (0.6 cm) seam allowance throughout, that means that you will stitch all your seams ¼" (0.6 cm) from the fabric edge.

Seam Ripper

A seam ripper is a tool used in a few different ways: to clip the threads in a seam to remove a few stitches, to undo a seam entirely, or to make an opening in the center of a stitched area, like a buttonhole.

Selvage Edge

The selvage is the narrow, tightly woven finished edge along each side of the lengthwise grain of your fabric.

Slipstitch

Frequently used to join two folded edges, slipstitching is nearly invisible as the thread is slipped under the fabric's fold. You'll need a long piece of thread and a sharp needle.

a. To begin, feed one end of the thread through the eye of the needle, doubling the thread back on itself. Match the cut ends and make a double knot.

b. Insert your needle into one piece of fabric, at the folded edge, coming up from the **wrong** side, and pull the thread taut, hiding the knot.

c. Then insert the needle through a few threads on the other edge of the fabric. Pull the thread through until it is taut.

d. Insert the needle back into the first side, through about ½" (1.3 cm) of the fabric, hiding the thread inside the fold. Push the needle through the fabric and again pull the thread taut.

e. Repeat this process until you have stitched your fabric together, keeping even spaces between stitches.

f. To finish, tie off your stitching by making a double knot close to the fabric and cut the extra thread.

Square Up

After stitching together a number of pieces, as in a quilt top, it can be important to trim away excess fabric to make the edges even and the corners right angles before continuing with the next step. See *Assembling the Quilt*.

Stay Stitching

A line of stay stitches might be sewn in the seam allowance while constructing your project. Stay stitching helps stabilize curved or slanted edges by keeping the fabric from stretching, and helps reinforce the fabric when making clips in the seam allowance.

Stitch-in-the-Ditch

This stitch, done by machine or hand, is sewn in the groove formed by a seam. Make sure to line up any seams underneath so both seams will be sewn through neatly. This creates almost invisible stitches, but draws attention to the outlines of the various pieces.

Template

A pattern piece used for tracing or for marking guidelines on your project.

Topstitch

Topstitching is used for several purposes. It finishes your project and gives it a neat appearance; it's used to close the opening after turning your project **right** side out; and it can be used as a reinforcement stitch. To topstitch, stitch parallel to an edge or a seam as suggested in the project's instructions.

Trim the Corners

This is a great finishing technique used to add shape and definition to corners on your project. Use your scissors to cut off the tip of the corner in the seam allowance to eliminate bulk. Be careful not to clip your stitching. Once you turn your project **right** side out, your corner will have a neat, squared-off look.

Trim the Seam Allowance

This technique reduces bulk along the seams, so they'll lie flat when you turn the project **right** side out. Use your scissors to cut off most of the excess fabric in the seam allowance. Be sure to press out these areas once you've turned your project **right** side out.

Turning Tool

A turning tool is a pointed object such as a closed pair of scissors that can be used to push out the corners on your project after you have turned it **right** side out. Specially made turning tools, usually constructed of plastic or wood, are available at sewing and fabric stores. When using a turning tool, push out the corners gently, especially if you are working with delicate, lightweight fabric.

Whipstitch

A whipstitch is a hand-sewing technique used to loosely close an opening or to keep pieces together. It will not usually show on the finished project. To whipstitch, make large overcast stitches, passing over the edge of the fabric diagonally.

Width of Fabric (WOF)

The measurement from selvage to selvage, or the crossgrain.

Resource Guide

Fabrics

See Amy's "Where to Buy" to find independent fabric shops worldwide— www.amybutlerdesign.com/buy

New Fabric Sources

Westminster/Coats— www.makeitcoats.com/en-us

FreeSpirit—http://freespiritfabric.com

Rowan Fabrics/Kaffe Fasset Collective— www.makeitcoats.com/en-us

Cotton + Steel— www.cottonandsteelfabrics.com

Moda Fabrics— http://storefront.unitednotions.com /storefrontCommerce

Liberty of London— www.liberty.co.uk/ fcpdepartmenthome/dept/fabrics

Seven Islands— www.sevenislandsfabric.com

Vintage fabric sources

Amazon—www.amazon.com

Ebay—www.ebay.com

Flea markets and shows www.brimfieldshow.com www.roundtop-marburger.com www.springfieldantiqueshow.com

Silk Sari Fabrics

Amazon—www.amazon.com

Ebay—www.ebay.com

Batting, Design Foam, Stabilizers, and Interfacings

Batting & Pillow Forms— Fairfield, www.fairfieldworld.com

Silk Batting—Hobb's Quilt Batting, www.hobbsbatting.com

Foamology Design Foam— http://foamology101.com

Interfacings—Pellon, www.pellonprojects.com

Heat Moldable Stabilizer—Bosal, www.bosalonline.com/bosal_ interfacing.html

Muslin and Canvas

James Thompson— www.jamesthompson.com

Quilting Supplies and Notions

Prym-Dritz— www.prym-consumer-usa.com/ brands/dritz

Zipperstop—www.zipperstop.com

JoAnn Fabrics & Crafts—www.joann.com

Amazon—www.amazon.com

Beads, Bead Caps, and Beading Supplies

MK Beads—www.mkbeads.com

Artbeads.com—www.artbeads.com

Fusion Beads—www.fusionbeads.com

Lima Beads—www.limabeads.com

Fire Mountain Gems & Beads— www.firemountaingems.com

Bead Paradise—www.beadparadise.com

Miyuki Beads— www.miyuki-beads.co.jp/english

Amazon—www.amazon.com

Threads and Embroidery Floss

All-purpose thread, Button & Carpet thread— www.makeitcoats.com/en-us

DMC Embroidery Floss & Pearl Cotton— www.dmc-usa.com

J&P Coats Embroidery Floss & Anchor Pearl Cotton— www.makeitcoats.com/en-us

Online Craft Stores

Hobby Lobby—www.hobbylobby.com

JoAnn Fabrics & Crafts—www.joann.com

Michael's Craft Store—www.michaels.com

Dick Blick's—www.dickblick.com

Home Furnishings and Decorative Objects

Target—www.target.com

Ikea—www.ikea.com

Tandy Leather Factory (leather strips)— www.tandyleatherfactory.com/en-usd/ home/home.aspx

Five Below—www.fivebelow.com

Amazon—www.amazon.com

Online Resources

www.mollyflanders.blogspot.com

www.ruthsinger.com

www.onlinequilter.com

www.beadwrangler.com/index.htm

www.sublimestitching.com

www.antiquequiltdating.com/index.html

www.smithsonianmag.com

www.womenfolk.com

www.dmc-usa.com

www.urbanthreads.com

www.fiberartnow.net

www.hartcottagequilts.com

www.antiquequiltdating.com

www.kamat.com/index.htm

Books

Reader's Digest Complete Guide to Sewing by Reader's Digest

Reader's Digest Complete Guide to Needlework by Reader's Digest

Material Obsession by Kathy Doughty and Sarah Fielke

The Ultimate Sashiko Sourcebook by Susan Briscoe

The Great American Log Cabin Quilt Book by Carol Anne Wien

Special Thanks

Many thanks to everyone who contributed to this book. It's my grandest pleasure to create with you!

   A special thanks to the following folks: To my husband, David Butler, for your loving support, imagination, and spunk! Your photographs make this book come alive! To Sheila, my friend, your hard work, patience, and creativity brought an amazing energy to this project. I am so proud of what we created. To Kerri Thomson, Mary Dugan, Molly Frye, and Alyssa Van Ausdal for your development prowess, problem solving, and beautiful project sewing! To Monique Keegan for your smiles and super talented styling abilities. To Danielle and Jason Bitner, and Miss Keegan, for allowing us to take photos in your gorgeous spaces. To Lauren Vannatta and Katie Tolerton, our lovely models who make the garments and accessories look amazing! To Westminster Fibers for shipping box after box of fabulous fabrics for me to play with: I appreciate your friendship and generosity. To these fine companies for supplying interfacings, batting, pillows, notions, and sewing tools: Prym Dritz, Pellon, Bosal, and Fairfield. To Dolin O'Shea for your much appreciated editing assistance, and to my friend and editor Amy Treadwell, for being my compass. Your support, patience, and encouragement mean the world to me.

Amy Butler

Index